THE BASICS OF BUDGETING

A Practical Guide to Better

Business Planning

Terry Dickey

A FIFTY-MINUTE™ SERIES BOOK

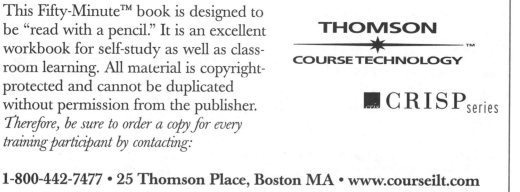

This Fifty-Minute™ book is designed to be "read with a pencil." It is an excellent workbook for self-study as well as classroom learning. All material is copyright-protected and cannot be duplicated without permission from the publisher. *Therefore, be sure to order a copy for every training participant by contacting:*

THOMSON
COURSE TECHNOLOGY™

■ CRISP series

1-800-442-7477 • 25 Thomson Place, Boston MA • www.courseilt.com

THE BASICS OF BUDGETING
A Practical Guide to Better Business Planning

Terry Dickey

CREDITS
Editor: **Tony Hicks**
Assistant Editor: **Genevieve McDermott**
Production Manager: **Denise Powers**
Designer: **Carol Harris**
Typesetting: **ExecuStaff**
Cover Design: **Nicole Phillips**

For more information contact:

Course Technology
25 Thomson Place
Boston, MA 02210

Or find us on the Web at **www.courseilt.com**

For permission to use material from this text or product, submit a request online at www.thomsonrights.com.

Trademarks
Crisp Learning is a trademark of Course Technology. Some of the product names and company names used in this book have been used for identification purposes only, and may be trademarks or registered trademarks of their respective manufacturers and sellers.

Disclaimer
Course Technology reserves the right to revise this publication and make changes from time to time in its content without notice.

ISBN 1-56052-134-1
Library of Congress Catalog Card Number 91-76241
Printed in Canada by Webcom Limited

8 9 10 PM 06 05 04

LEARNING OBJECTIVES FOR:

THE BASICS OF BUDGETING

The objectives for *The Basics of Budgeting* are listed below. They have been developed to guide you, the reader, to the core issues covered in this book.

Objectives

- ❑ 1) **To discuss principles of strategic planning**

- ❑ 2) **To show how to budget sales, labor, depreciation and other expenses**

- ❑ 3) **To review financial and presentation aspects of budget plans**

Assessing Your Progress

In addition to the learning objectives above, Course Technology has developed a Crisp Series **assessment** that covers the fundamental information presented in this book. A 25-item, multiple-choice and true/false questionnaire allows the reader to evaluate his or her comprehension of the subject matter. To buy the assessment and answer key, go to www.courseilt.com and search on the book title or via the assessment format, or call 1-800-442-7477.

Assessments should not be used in any employee selection process.

ABOUT THIS BOOK

In modern business, good planning skills are fundamental to success.

FOR LARGE CORPORATIONS, planning is the only way to control many people doing lots of different things. In large companies, it is no longer the responsibility of a few senior managers. Scores of people, most with other responsibilities, are involved in building plans and budgets. Skill in this area has become very important to career advancement.

SMALL BUSINESSES also need strong planning skills. In small businesses, the margin for error is small, and there are few second chances. Success is difficult, even with top-notch planning skills. Without them, luck simply isn't enough.

However, planning skills are hard to develop. Most people practice only once per year. The newer, leaner corporation has few people to teach the skills, and the typical small business has no resources at all.

Everyone preaches the virtues of planning, but few people know how to do it. Even fewer know how to do it *well*. This book will give you sound, proven skills that will be "portable" between positions and employers. Such skills will contribute greatly to your ultimate business success.

CONTENTS

INTRODUCTION

The Basics of Budgeting is for people who want better business planning skills. Among others, it is intended for corporate managers, small-business owners, students, new analysts, and business veterans who want to sharpen planning skills.

This is not the usual "budget book." It is not theoretical, and it is not an exhaustive text. Instead, it explains fundamental concepts in a way that is clear, practical and "street wise." The tips and techniques have been proven in actual companies in the real world. They really work.

This book also includes examples of calculations. They are simple and easy to follow. They show how to approach common problems and are useful as models for good presentation form. If you use a computer, you may want to prop the book next to the keyboard, and use the examples as templates for your own planning models.

A great deal of this book shows how to plan income statements and departmental expenses. Although balance-sheet and cash-flow planning is best left to finance professionals, there is a reference chapter on these topics.

One of the biggest obstacles to planning success is the planning process itself. Whether managing a company-wide effort or planning a departmental budget, you will find useful insights about the *process*, and how to make it work for you, your career and your business.

Although this material is not complex, it will take time and effort to master. If you need immediate help, skim the table of contents and go directly to the appropriate area. Otherwise, study the book in the order it is written. That way, each section can build on earlier ones. Good luck!

Jerry Dickey

HOW TO USE THIS BOOK

This book is organized to make the planning process easy to understand. Although you do not need to be an accountant to benefit from it, it assumes you can recognize the major parts of financial statements, and that you have at least some idea of what various accounts contain.* Particular parts of this book will mean more to you, right now, than others. However, over the course of your business career, it is likely you will need them all.

Most people are responsible for small parts of a big budget, or else they are responsible for managing a planning process for an entire company. This material will be useful for both. However, since each group has a different amount of control, each will draw different lessons from this information. The examples come from both situations.

It's a good strategy to work straight through, in the order in which the book is written, since each part builds on the other. Here is a preview:

Parts 1–3 deal with how to manage *the planning process as a whole:* what it is, how it works, and how to plan effectively and efficiently.

Part 4 deals with *strategic plans.* Strategic planning is not just for companies; even individual departments need a strategic plan. A good strategic plan keeps the organization oriented toward long-term goals.

Parts 5–10 deal with *the annual operating plan,* what most companies call a "budget." These parts also contain examples of calculations needed for financial projections. The examples will work for strategic plans, annual operating plans and forecasts, with minor modifications.

*If you would like to brush up your accounting skills, you might find another Crisp publication, *Understanding Financial Statements,* by James Gill, very useful.

Part 11 is a reference chapter. It deals with *balance-sheet and cash-flow planning*. Small-business owners already know the importance of cash flow. Although most corporate managers don't worry much about balance sheets, at some point in their career they will. For both, this is a useful introduction to an important topic.

Parts 12–14 cover *budget reviews, budget processes and adjusted plans*. These parts are mainly for those who are designing a budget process, or for those who must submit budgets to an outside review.

Part 15 deals with *forecasts and control*. It shows how to create quick and accurate forecasts, and how to improve business control.

IMPORTANT. Financial planning skills are powerful, but they can be misused. Never take any action which can expose you or your firm to financial or other risk until you have discussed it thoroughly with competent professional counsel. The financial statements described in this book are for illustration purposes only, and do not necessarily reflect typical financials for the businesses indicated. All firms and individuals are fictitious, and do not represent actual people or organizations.

P A R T

I

Basic Information

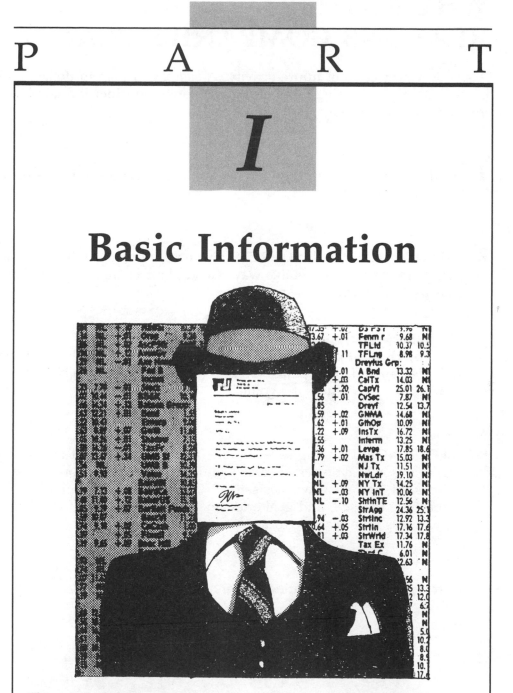

This part of the book is an easy read. It is important for three reasons. First, it will acquaint you with the vocabulary and common practices of planning. Second, it will give you a good background for the rest of the book. Finally, it will help you work the budget process—a key component of planning skill.

WHY BOTHER?
REASONS COMPANIES PLAN

A *plan* is a projection of future activity. A *budget* is a plan in dollars and cents. Although planning takes effort, companies consider it a good investment. Here is why:

1. **CONTROL.** Plans are the foundation of business control. The only alternative is chaos.

2. **ALLOCATION OF RESOURCES.** Businesses prosper when they use assets in the most profitable way. Good plans change the way businesses use assets, which increases profits.

3. **OUTSIDE RESPONSIBILITIES.** Investors, banks, shareholders and boards demand good plans. No one wants to invest in a firm that has no ''firm'' idea where it's going.

4. **EFFICIENCY.** Planning saves time, effort, and money. It lets managers make mistakes *on paper*. It creates an inventory of decisions made, issues discussed, and controversies settled. Organizations that plan are proactive, focused, and goal-oriented. They fight fewer ''fires'' and spend less time reacting to unpleasant surprises.

Tried, true, and worth repeating is Planner's Rule #1:

> **PLANNER'S RULE #1:**
> **WHEN YOU FAIL TO PLAN, YOU PLAN TO FAIL.**

THE PLANNING CYCLE

Each year businesses create, monitor and execute business plans. This process is called the *planning cycle*. Here is a brief description of that process:

STRATEGIC PLAN. The *strategic plan* is the first step. It represents deep, long-term thinking about the most important questions that face the firm. Typical questions: What is the real mission of this firm? What is the ultimate goal? What does the future look like? How must we change to prosper there? Financial projections are general, and the plan usually covers five years.

ANNUAL OPERATING PLAN. Next, the firm turns to the coming year. This detailed blueprint for the immediate future is the *annual operating plan*. It is what most companies mean when they refer to their "budget." Financial projections are very detailed.

ADJUSTED PLAN. After the year actually starts, things change. If the business changes too rapidly, it outgrows the plan. Often, firms formally change it, producing an *adjusted plan*. This keeps the variance between actual and planned performance meaningful.

FORECASTS are informal projections done during the year. Often, firms forecast year-end results when the company is half-way through the year. Some create a new forecast each month. These are usually quick, fairly simple processes.

BUSINESS PLANS, in the specific sense, are fairly standard documents that organizations use to apply for venture capital, etc. They are very similar to strategic plans, but are usually more detailed.

THE PLANNING CYCLE (continued)

Your company probably does similar things but uses different words. This book always uses the words as defined above.

Describe the planning cycle in your company. When do these events usually occur? Write your answer in the space below.

_____

_____

_____

_____

_____

_____

_____

_____

_____

_____

_____

_____

_____

_____

PLANNER'S RULE #2:

ALWAYS KNOW WHICH KIND OF PLAN YOU WANT TO BUILD.

THE BASIC EQUATION

All plans are made the same way. At the lowest level, each part of a plan is a simple equation. It is:

DATA + ASSUMPTIONS = PROJECTIONS

Data are facts: statements about the past you *know* to be true.
Assumptions are beliefs: statements about the future you *believe* will come true.
Projections are the result of applying assumptions to data.

An example: Last year, sales were $1 million (data). They will grow 15% (assumption). Therefore, sales will be $1.15 million (projection).

Rule number 1. Always keep a *short, logical connection* between data, assumptions and projections. Don't make a daisy chain of projections based on other projections.

Rule number 2. Strive for *balance.* Continually ask: ''Which is weaker, the data or the assumptions?'' Then concentrate on that area. Don't be like the individual with stacks of historical computer reports but very fuzzy ideas about the future. On the other hand, don't try to overcome flimsy historical data with lots of elaborate assumptions about the future.

List three informal statements about the future (projections) you have heard recently. Identify the data and assumptions behind each one.

	Projections	=	Data	+	Assumptions
1.	_____		_____		_____
2.	_____		_____		_____
3.	_____		_____		_____

Start with data you know to be true. Build a daisy chain (data plus assumptions equals projections, plus another assumption equals a further projection, etc.). How long does it take to reach a ridiculous conclusion?

Data	+	Assumption	=	Projection
_____		_____		_____
		Additional Assumption	=	Resulting Projection
		_____		_____
		_____		_____
		_____		_____

FOUR NECESSARY WAYS TO PRESENT EVERY PLAN

Like a pyramid with four sides, any plan can be viewed four ways. Good presentations always cover them all. They are: *discussion, financials, economics, and business indicators.*

1. DISCUSSION. This is "the story," the description in *words* behind the numbers. Who are you? What happened in the past? Why do you need money? Why do you exist? Where will you be in the future? What are you going to do? Why is that important? How will you be more-better-cheaper-faster? If a key decision maker is not a financial guru, can he or she still understand what you want?

2. FINANCIALS. Review past financial statements and project future ones.

3. ECONOMICS. Review and project the *economic* numbers behind the plan. How many people will it take? How many square feet of manufacturing space? How many product units will be sold? Hours of service billed? How many customers? etc.

4. BUSINESS INDICATORS tell the "story behind the story." Although financials tell *if* a plan is achieved, business indicators tell *how.* Often dividing a financial number by an economic number creates a business indicator. Unit price is an example—total dollars (financial number) divided by total units sold (economic number) gives price, or dollars per unit (business indicator). Others might be sales per employee, or sales per same-age-location. *Every function everywhere has a half-dozen business indicators that paint a complete picture of what is going on.* Can you list yours?

1. _____

2. _____

3. _____

4. _____

5. _____

6. _____

Context is vital. Never present a plan without a good historical foundation. Use the same four means to cover history: words, economics and indicators. Generally, look as far into the past as the projections extend into the future. Design financial schedules so that history and projections are easily scanned on the same page.

> **PLANNER'S RULE #3:**
>
> **DESCRIBE PLANS ALL FOUR WAYS, WITH ADEQUATE HISTORICAL CONTEXT.**

PLANNING PHILOSOPHIES

Many companies have specific (and sometimes peculiar) ways they develop and evaluate plans. This reflects their *planning philosophy*. Here are a few examples, from the thousands available.

SALES BUDGETS. The right way to project sales varies widely from industry to industry and company to company. Many take a historical approach; others plan by customer; some by geography, by market size and share, etc. The variations are countless, and different ones may be just as valid as the ones actually used.

VARIABLE BUDGETS. Expense budgets are expressed as a percentage of sales, instead of in absolute dollars.

LINE-ITEM BUDGETS. The budget is a long "laundry list" of items which will be evaluated one by one.

ZERO-BASED BUDGETS. This is an approach for staff and overhead budgets. It usually means three budgets: one at present activity levels, one at 20% less activity, and one at 20% more (the percentages may vary). Senior managers rank the resulting decision packages. They strike a "funding line" across the list to eliminate packages which don't qualify. ("Zero-based" sometimes means only an aggressive evaluation, not a true ZBB philosophy.)

HISTORICAL TREND BUDGETS. To grow sales by a certain percentage versus the previous year, and evaluate expenses by the size of increase.

FUND BUDGETS. This philosophy plans in categories which are fixed by law or executive decision. Examples include governments that must spend a certain tax only on road improvement, or a company that budgets $10 million on research and development, without knowing exactly what projects will be launched.

STRESS BUDGETS. This philosophy is not about money; it is about employee evaluation. Intentionally, the demands are tough, the time is short, and the review is horrendous. The goal is to "shoot the weaklings" and "keep the survivors."

Does your organization have a particular budget philosophy about any group of expenses—sales for example? Describe it.

_____

_____

_____

_____

Identify strengths and weaknesses of the budget philosophies listed below. Include any other philosophy you have encountered.

	Strengths	Weaknesses
Sales philosophies	_____	_____
Variable budgets	_____	_____
Line-item budgets	_____	_____
Zero-based budgets	_____	_____
Historical trend budgets	_____	_____
Fund budgets	_____	_____
Stress budgets	_____	_____
Any other philosophy you've encountered:		
_____	_____	_____
_____	_____	_____
_____	_____	_____

Do you have a preference? Why? _____

_____

Regardless of which philosophy a company uses, the techniques in this book are basic to them all. Organizations that have a strong commitment to a particular philosophy usually provide thorough indoctrination as part of normal training.

PLANNER'S RULE #4

KNOW YOUR COMPANY'S BUDGET PHILOSOPHY, AND ADAPT TO IT.

SUMMARY OF PART 1

Plans are important because they control what an organization does and how it allocates resources. They also aid communication with outside interests. An annual *planning cycle* produces four different kinds of plans: a *strategic plan*, an *annual operating plan*, an *adjusted plan* and *various forecasts*. Plans are built from a basic equation: data + assumptions = projections. Keep data and assumptions balanced, and the logical connection short. Plans should be presented four ways: discussion, financials, economics and business indicators. Always provide adequate historical context in plan presentations. Always know the budget philosophy of your particular organization.

Effective Planning in Your Organization

Jim was a graduate from a leading business school, a vice-president, successful, fast-track and in trouble. Several weeks ago he sent his budget package back to the finance department, with the comment that he was too busy. Could they do it for him? They did.

Now Jim was two hours out from a review with the company president. He had too little money, no clue about what he had asked for, and a newly acquired understanding of how seriously budgets were viewed in the company.

The material on the following pages might have been of use to him. . . .

A PLAN IS A SOCIAL DOCUMENT

The easiest way to fail in budgeting is to retreat to a dark corner with a personal computer and wait for supernatural inspiration. A *plan is a social document*, produced in a society, which is the organization. It has rules, regulations, rewards, penalties, and methods of communication. Ignore them at your peril! Always consider *at least* the following individuals:

► **SUPERVISORS.** What do they want from your budgets? How important are the budgets to them? How much effort do they want you to give to them? What agendas do they have that may not be published? What are their goals for your performance? What are the requirements of investors? Of banks or other financing groups?

► **PEERS.** What do people in other departments think about important issues facing the company? Are there managers or entrepreneurs with similar interests, problems, or concerns? What do they know that can improve your plan?

► **SUBORDINATES.** Good insights come from everywhere. Bring in the best thinking of *all* the people you work with.

► **PEOPLE OUTSIDE THE COMPANY.** What insight can customers give about future sales? Suppliers about future prices? How about industry, trade or professional groups? How about competitors? What are the planning implications of local and national economic trends? Of general business news?

Become an information sponge. Involve everyone you can. Listen.

In your planning, what needs must you satisfy for each of the groups listed below? And what planning resources can each group provide?

	They need:	They can provide:
Supervisors, bankers, financiers and board members		
Peers, other managers and other business owners		
Subordinates		

However, your budget is your professional lifeline. Involvement is one thing, but control is something entirely different. Never give control of your lifeline to anyone else.

PLANNER'S RULE #5

NEVER PLAN ALONE (BUT ALWAYS KEEP CONTROL).

STANDARDS OF PRECISION

Generally, planning standards are looser than accounting standards. Companies vary widely in how precise plans are required to be. Dollars may be rounded to the nearest thousand, or million. Intricate depreciation and tax rules may be simplified. The company may choose not to plan for every single account, or even every single organization.

Managers who stay up late to project to the nearest dollar when everyone else is rounding to *thousands*, won't be effective in their organization. Nor will managers who round to *ten thousands* when everyone else is rounding to *thousands*.

> **PLANNER'S RULE #6**
>
> **KNOW THE ACCEPTED STANDARD OF PRECISION.**

It may sometimes pay to use a different standard. That requires judgment. However, that decision is not difficult, once managers realize that they can—and should—make it deliberately.

Identify the accepted standard of precision for plans in your organization.

_____

What would be the advantages of planning at a more detailed level?

_____

_____

What would be the disadvantages?

_____

_____

What would be the advantages of planning at a more general level?

_____

_____

What would be the disadvantages?

_____

_____

LINE AND LEVEL OF CONTROL

Companies also vary in what *parts* of plans are important, and in *who* is responsible for achieving plans. Managers at certain *levels* are responsible for particular *lines* on financial statements.

The key *level* in an organization might be vice-presidents, department heads, or store managers. The key *lines* might be ''bottom-line profit,'' or ''sales and profit,'' or even every single line on the income statement.

Does upper management care about *how* profit is achieved? Is there freedom to go over on one account and under on another?

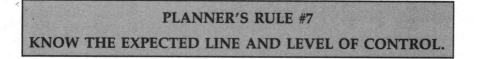

PLANNER'S RULE #7

KNOW THE EXPECTED LINE AND LEVEL OF CONTROL.

Like the standard of precision, the line and level of control should be a deliberate decision.

- If low-level employees are worried about unimportant variances instead of doing their job, the line and level may both be too low.

- If senior managers can't tell what happened when the plan is missed—if they are continually surprised by plan variances—then the line and level may both be too high.

Always remember that *your* part of the organization may have different needs than the organization as a whole.

Identify the line and level of control in your organization.

Line(s) on financial statement   *Controlled by*

_____   _____

_____   _____

_____   _____

How would your organization change, given a different line and level of control?

_____

_____

THE INFORMATION FRONTIER

Between the summarized information in financial statements and the overwhelming detail of a single transaction, an organization runs out of its ability to know. This is the *information frontier.*

Suppose you have to plan sales. You may only know total sales; or you may know sales by product line; or you may know:

- sales by product line and by distribution channel

- sales by product line, by distribution channel and by geographical area

- sales by product line, by distribution channel, by geographical area and by customer group

Whatever the company knows, to be successful in planning, you must know *what the company knows plus one level more.*

> **PLANNER'S RULE #8**
>
> **PLAN ONE LEVEL BEYOND THE INFORMATION FRONTIER.**

Managers who work one level beyond are smarter than anyone else in a budget review. They demonstrate the mastery of someone closer to the action. They plug into trends they would otherwise miss, their budgets are more accurate, and their businesses are more successful.

Find the information frontier by examining routine reports. What is the finest level of detail they show? Is useful information buried in the cubicle of that strange person no one ever talks to? What kind of informal reporting is needed from subordinates to reach one level beyond?

Now write your answers to these questions:

What is the information frontier in your organization for sales?

_____

For payroll expenses?

_____

What would it take to go one level beyond?

_____

What are the advantages of doing that?

_____

_____

The disadvantages?

_____

_____

RULES FOR JUNGLE FIGHTERS

Budgeting is an imperfect art and competition for dollars is intense. Sly veterans and devious subordinates often turn into vicious jungle fighters to preserve budget empires and get projects funded. To cope, managers need to understand the rules of jungle warfare. Here are a few:

1. **COOPERATE THE RIGHT AMOUNT.** Budget cutters start with areas they know well and also areas where they feel suspicious. If they know about all your wiggle room, but not about anyone else's, guess who loses? On the other hand, if they know too little, you'll end up with a 15% reduction while everyone else gets only 5%. Jungle fighters cooperate the right amount.

2. **PAD THE HIERARCHY.** If a company rolls the budget up from the lowest level in the company, jungle fighters in the middle shave performance levels at every step to make the plan easier to hit. On the other hand, if the budget rolls down from senior management, jungle fighters increase the performance expected from their subordinates. Either way increases their own wiggle room.

3. **SPEND AND COMMIT—EARLY.** Companies start the year with high hopes and a new plan. Midway through, they are often short of plan and are cutting costs. After a few repeat years, such companies breed jungle fighters who spend budgets in the first half of the year. Reductions have to come from someone else.

4. **PLAN EARLY, SPEND LATE.** Some jungle fighters plan to hire individuals early in the year, but actually delay it as long as possible. This produces a positive expense variance that can hide a number of things.

5. **OFFER THE UNTHINKABLE.** When pressed to trim costs, jungle fighters offer the most important thing they control. Obviously, everything else is even more important, so other budgets must be cut first.

6. **ASK FOR THE ABSURD AND SETTLE FOR THE FANTASTIC.** When jungle fighters need a 5% increase, they ask for 15%. When management takes 5% off everyone's budget, the jungle fighter takes an afternoon off to figure out how to spend the extra funds.

There are thousands of jungle fighter techniques. These are just a few. What would you add to the list?

_____

_____

The good planner doesn't need them and doesn't tolerate them in others. However, in organizations that breed jungle fighters, survivors know the rules. What approaches would you use to defeat these tactics?

1. If someone cooperates only the "right" amount:

_____

2. If someone pads the hierarchy:

_____

3. If someone spends and commits early:

_____

4. If someone plans early and spends late:

_____

5. If someone offers the unthinkable:

_____

6. If someone asks for the absurd:

_____

7. Other tactics:

_____

_____

_____

_____

_____

SUMMARY OF PART 2

Planning effectively in your organization involves several survival techniques. Plug into the organization, learn what everyone wants from the process, and figure out how they can help you. Never plan alone, but always keep control. Know the expected standard of precision and the accepted line and level of control. Find the information frontier, and always plan one level beyond it. Be aware of the rules for jungle fighters when planning in troubled organizations.

P A R T

3

How to Build
Plans Efficiently

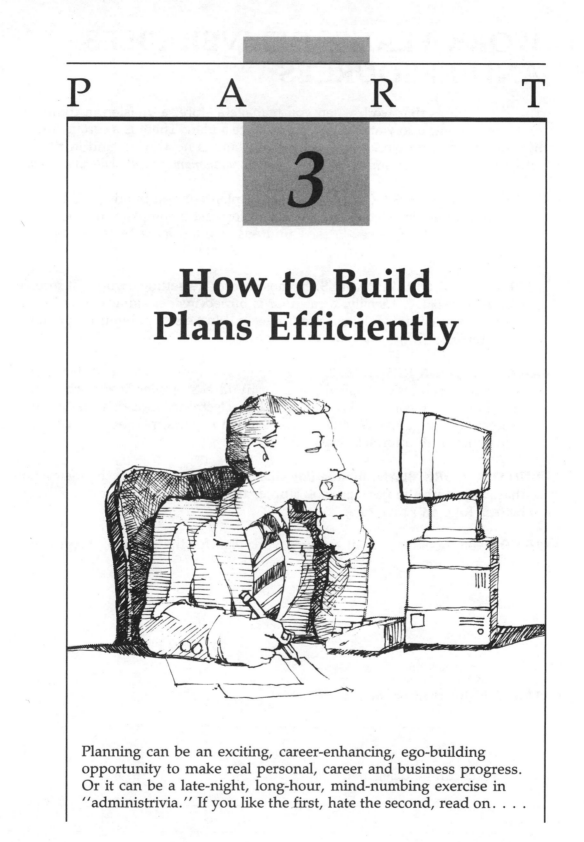

Planning can be an exciting, career-enhancing, ego-building opportunity to make real personal, career and business progress. Or it can be a late-night, long-hour, mind-numbing exercise in "administrivia." If you like the first, hate the second, read on. . . .

WORK PLANS, DELIVERABLES AND RESOURCES

The same things that work when you manage a store, a division, a company or a department, also work when you produce a plan. There is a certain amount of brute production work in any plan, and there is no way around it. So, when faced with a planning task, *don't check your management skills at the door.*

THINK ABOUT THE GOAL. What kind of plan are you building? What is the appropriate level of detail? Must you forecast a complete income statement? Just a few key lines? Hundreds of financial statements? Do you need month-by-month detail, or just annual totals?

ISOLATE THE DELIVERABLES. In most corporate settings, you will receive a budget package. Usually, a calendar is buried inside, along with a list of items you must do or deliver. Ignore everything else until you isolate these deliverables.

ANALYZE YOUR RESOURCES. Budgeting for a typical overhead department is a fairly small task. Detailed plans for hundreds of sites is a much larger one. Look for resources. Who is skilled on electronic spreadsheets or word processing programs? Who are the unknown experts, perhaps with budget experience with a former employer?

BUILD A WORK PLAN. Build a flowchart to plan the work. If the instructions that came with the package look stupid, they probably are. Do something better. Take an active role.

Use the space below to draft a rough work plan for the planning process in your organization.

How can this plan be improved?

_____

_____

What parts can be delegated?

_____

_____

THE SECRET OF THE FIVE-MINUTE BUDGET

The first "professional secret" good planners learn is the five-minute solution: *No matter what the problem, force an answer within five minutes.* Then look at the pieces, figure out the uncertainties, and use remaining time to reduce them, in order of importance.

Look at the benefits.

- Effort is structured. You know what you are doing, and why.

- Efficiency increases. Time isn't spent where it won't make a difference.

- Focus improves. You never lose the big picture.

- Results are realistic. The twenty-minute solution, the one-day solution and the two-week solution may be very different, but each must justify itself against the earlier one. No one spends two weeks developing absurd answers.

A plan is an example of a five-minute problem. Suppose a division will do $1 million in sales this year; the cost of sales is 50%; and expenses are $250,000. For next year, the best judgment of sales growth is 15%. These are the calculations you need to do:

Sales budget ($1 million + 15%): $1,150,000.

Cost of sales (50% of $1,150,000) should be $575,000.

An additional rep will be needed, at $30,000 a year, so expenses will be $250,000 + $30,000 = $280,000.

The resulting profit ($575,000 − $280,000) is $295,000.

Presto—a five-minute budget.

THE FIVE-MINUTE BUDGET (continued)

Now take any problem you are facing and force a five-minute solution.

_____

_____

_____

_____

_____

Identify the areas of uncertainty.

_____

_____

_____

_____

_____

Which is most in need of additional work? Put a check next to it. What would you do next?

_____

_____

_____

_____

_____

Successive revision is important. No one stakes a career on a five-minute answer, so select the most uncertain element and repeat the process. Continue until the level of risk is acceptable, or you hit the information frontier.

Reality checks are also important. Every time you achieve a new result, compare it to the previous answer. Convince yourself that any changes are valid, before proceeding. Then use that revised number as the new reality check. This will save countless hours by catching easily detectable errors.

A RESOURCE CHECKLIST

You can plan more efficiently by collecting information all at once. Every company has information which can make planning easier. In a corporate environment, if you are lucky, it may be in the budget package. In small businesses—again, if you are lucky—it may only need to be collected.

You may not be lucky. You may need to locate it yourself. Figure out what you need, survey the company, and take appropriate steps. Following is a checklist; use it as a starting point, then build your own by adding or deleting items as appropriate.

CHECKLIST OF RESOURCES

Personnel Department:
Description of pay grades and salary ranges
Current compensation policy
Policies on promotion, merit, and cost-of-living
    increases
Details on union agreements, if applicable
Wage, salary, tax, and benefits planning tools
Details about cost of current benefit programs
Details of current bonus programs
Organizational structure and headcount

_____

_____

Finance Department:
Historical financial statements
Check registers and trial balance reports
Chart of accounts with an explanation of each
Accounting policies on relevant areas (accruals,
    depreciation, amortization, allocated expenses, etc.)
Capital asset register, or equivalent (assets, purchase
    date, monthly and cumulative depreciation)
Copies of spreadsheet models that can help
Hierarchy of cost and profit centers

_____

_____

CHECKLIST OF RESOURCES (continued)

Marketing Department:
Historical sales reports (detailed and summarized)
Explanation of future market trends
Details of sales promotions and probable effects for next year
Sales projections

_____

_____

Those managing the budget process:
Economic assumptions (growth, inflation, etc.)
General goals and expectations about your particular budget
List of items you must provide to complete the process
Calendar listing key due dates
How and when to calendarize from annual totals
Budget evaluation philosophy
Structure and timing of budget reviews
Additional resources available to you

_____

_____

Your boss:
Goals for your department or function
Expectations for plan results
Any hidden agendas
Understanding of what you must do to support him or her

_____

_____

People who report to you:
Goals for your department or function
Ideas that might not have occurred to you
Previous experience which can help
Agreement on what they must do to support you

_____

_____

Your peers: Informal consensus on issues facing the business.
                    Access to their planning experience.

_____

_____

Any other source: _____

_____

_____

_____

_____

_____

_____

_____

_____

_____

Identify three planning veterans in your present organization you can use
as mentors:

1. _____

2. _____

3. _____

SUMMARY OF PART 3

Companies vary widely in the amount of planning effort they require. Therefore, isolate the deliverables and understand exactly what has to be done. Build a work plan and identify all resources which can help do the job. Always start with a five-minute solution and use successive revision to stay focused. Build a resource checklist and gather information before building the plan.

P A R T

4

How to Build
a Strategic Plan

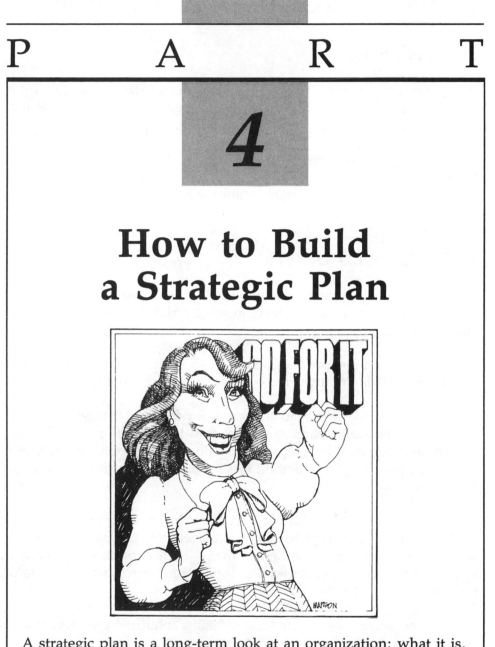

A strategic plan is a long-term look at an organization: what it is,
what it does and how it should change over the coming years.
All organizations need a strategic plan. Even if you only manage
a department, and even if your firm doesn't require one, do one
for your function anyway. It orients the department, with respect
to the company and the world at large. It keeps annual budgets
consistent with ultimate goals. It forces the long-term changes
that are necesasry for success.

HOW LONG AND WHO DOES IT?

TIME HORIZON

A strategic plan should look to the outer limit of the foreseeable future. A five-year plan works well for many firms. Further in the future is too uncertain; a shorter time provides too little guidance.

However, your needs might be different. Look at your product cycle. A timber company that needs 20 years to harvest a crop might need a 20-year plan. An importer dealing in consumer fads might need an 18-month plan. Decide on an appropriate time horizon.

WHO SHOULD DO IT?

Strategic direction for the company *must flow down* the organization from senior management, so the highest-level managers should create the strategic plan.

- They should seclude themselves in an informal setting for two days to a week. This improves focus, and frees them from distractions.

- The group should be small enough for free and efficient work—ten or fewer. Generally, support staff should be limited—probably one or two, to take minutes, intercept phone calls, run computer models, etc. This keeps planning from getting lost in details, posturing and inhibited discussion.

However, *strategic ideas should flow up,* from the lowest levels in the organization, so don't limit the concept to senior management. If they spend a week doing strategic planning for the entire company, each department could certainly spend a half day, doing something similar for their function. It could also feed the higher process.

If everyone spends deliberate time thinking about the long term, the results can be magic.

THE MISSION STATEMENT

The strategic plan should start with a *mission statement.* In one sentence, state what the organization does and why it exists. The mission statement should also indicate the industry, the geographical area, and the unique competitive advantage or niche.

Don't be surprised if this is difficult and takes a lot of time to develop. To break down mental roadblocks, think what customers, employees and suppliers would say. Seize every opportunity to redefine the organization in ways that are specific, active and market-oriented.

Think carefully about how narrow to make the mission. A *focused* mission statement leads firms to strongly push their unique competitive advantages. On the other hand, *broad* mission statements can lead to powerful new possibilities.

Here are some examples.

- Bent-Nail Builders supplies affordable housing to first-time purchasers in the tristate area.

- The Audio-Visual Department improves the effectiveness of sales communications and employee development at a significant savings over outside contractors.

- It's-A-Long-Way-To-Temporaries, Inc., provides temporary accounting help to firms that demand immediate service and premium quality in the metropolitan area.

A good mission statement truly defines the firm and strongly influences all it does.

PLANNER'S RULE #9

MISSION STATEMENTS: HAVE ONE.

YOUR ORGANIZATION'S MISSION STATEMENT

Write your organization's mission statement here:

_____

_____

_____

_____

_____

_____

_____

_____

_____

_____

_____

_____

_____

_____

_____

_____

_____

_____

_____

ANALYZING THE EXTERNAL ENVIRONMENT

Next, forget the firm, and focus on everything else. What will the future look like? Here are some typical places to start:

MARKETS. How big is the ultimate market? What trends are detectable in that market? Is the customer base growing? What is the expected market share? Will it go up or down? What are competitors doing? Is it time to move to international markets?

THE INDUSTRY. What are the direct competitors? The indirect competitors in related businesses? What are their prospects, plans, trends? What surprises could they have in store?

TECHNOLOGY. What technological changes will affect the organization? Are new production processes or future automation on the horizon?

GOVERNMENT. What trends are developing at the local, state and national levels? What does the future hold for regulation, liability and government policy changes?

CULTURE. What does the future hold for the hearts, minds, fads, fashions, habits, views, and actions of society as a whole?

ECONOMICS AND DEMOGRAPHICS. Where is the economy headed? Will the next five years be recessionary or expansionary? What will happen to interest rates, capital investment, macroeconomic growth? What will happen to age, income and the basic variables that affect the population as a whole?

ANALYZING THE EXTERNAL ENVIRONMENT (continued)

Of course, after every question, there is an obvious follow-up: *what does that mean to the organization?* Add any categories and strategic questions that are appropriate to your particular organization:

_____

_____

_____

_____

_____

List the top five external issues facing your organization:

1. _____

_____

_____

2. _____

_____

_____

3. _____

_____

_____

4. _____

_____

_____

5. _____

_____

_____

ANALYZING INTERNAL CAPABILITIES

Next, examine the organization. What are its strengths, its weaknesses? Rank them by importance. Flex each one, play what-if, brainstorm. Tear the organization into its major parts, and again into its major businesses. What if you could leave one part behind? What if you could expand another? Redefine another? What if the firm didn't have to worry about capital? What if it didn't depend on one major supplier? What if it were in two cities, not one? What if the department were cut in half? Doubled in size? What if a department went after external customers as well as internal ones?

By category:

MARKETING. What does the future hold for advertising, promotion, staffing, innovation, adaptability of the firm and its businesses?

FINANCE. Examine the basics: paying bills, collecting money, reporting. Are they adequate for the future? What should change? What should change in capital structure? Can growth be controlled?

PRODUCTION. Will costs remain competitive? What about suppliers? Labor contracts? Technology? Automation? Does the future hold new plants, plant relocations, more or less subcontracting or abandonment of production?

INFORMATION. Where are the information bottlenecks? What major systems will be developed? Will hardware, software and people resources be available to implement them?

ADMINISTRATION. Can expansions be managed? What are the weaknesses in the pool of executive talent?

PERSONNEL. What are the implications of government regulations? Employee morale? What changes in costs, contracts, benefits are in store? How about incentive compensation programs? Management and employee development? Wage and salary positioning versus the national market?

ANALYZING INTERNAL CAPABILITIES
(continued)

Add any categories and strategic questions that are appropriate to your organization. Do not forget to ask the questions of each major organization, and each business activity, product line, etc., as well as the firm as a whole.

_____

_____

_____

_____

_____

_____

List the top five internal issues facing your organization.

1. _____

_____

_____

2. _____

_____

_____

3. _____

_____

_____

4. _____

_____

_____

5. _____

_____

_____

PUTTING IT ALL TOGETHER

► **Work back and forth.** Cycle through the internal capabilities analysis steps until a clear view of the future emerges. Then do contingency planning.

What three things could kill the future? What then? It is no crime to bet the company, as long as that is an intentional decision.

Crank through several different financial projections. What do they look like if things don't work out?

Repeat, but with things turning wildly favorable. How much success can the firm afford?

► **Describe the future.** When the smoke has cleared, describe clearly and concisely what the future holds. Add majority and minority opinions, if necessary. Then:

► **Do financial projections.** Gather up the highest-level, most summarized financial statements available for the past five years. Project them out for the time horizon of the strategic plan, using the view of the future you have developed. At a minimum, these statements should include, for each year:

- Income statements
- Balance sheets
- Cash-flow statements

(A corporate department in most companies will only have a projected statement of expenses.) Keep projections high-level and summarized. A strategic plan always looks at the forest, never at the trees. (Techniques for doing financial calculations are described in Parts 6–11.)

► **Economics and business indicators.** Don't neglect to include microeconomic figures like headcount, number of units sold, etc. and also the business indicators like customer count, unit price, dollars per mature store, etc.

► **Write it down.** Summarize the results in a confidential memorandum. Large companies with mature planning processes might need an entire bookshelf to hold the plan and supporting data. Small firms, just starting the process, might need only a single page. A brief example somewhere between these extremes is shown on the next page.

EXAMPLE

MISSION

Joe's Barbecue is the preferred food-service choice for premium barbecued meats in the industrial district and middle-income neighborhoods in the southwest part of the city of Pinechip, Ohio. "Premium" means unique taste, unexcelled quality, and commanding top prices. "Preferred" means the dollar and unit volume leader in the defined market by a clear and dominant margin.

ANALYSIS OF THE EXTERNAL ENVIRONMENT

Culture and Demographics

Consumers will shift preference for the kind of meats they want. The average age of residents in the service area is advancing. This means fewer kids, and older customers. Trends toward eating a wider variety of foods will continue.

Economics

Lunch customers are mostly from the industrial district; 75% come from a single government contractor. This could pose a risk if future contracts are lost. Customers tend to eat out more when the economy slows down, so there appears to be no risk to the business from recession. No unusual risk is foreseen, due to advancing interest rates.

Competition

A new mall will open within 24 months; it will have sites for three food-service providers. Grocery stores appear to be expanding deli departments to include more barbecue. Sam's Barbecue will probably be taken over by the owner's son within three years; they will become more price-driven competitors.

Government

The highway commission plans road construction which will restrict access to the restaurant for six months, two years from now. Building codes will require $10,000 to upgrade plumbing at the current site, within 18 months.

Technology

Automated, microwave smokers designed for single-site restaurants will be available within the next five years. This could improve efficiency of this restaurant, but could also make entry into the business easier for new competitors.

Suppliers

Meat purchased for barbecuing follows commodity markets. Although the price varies widely, profit margins can be maintained well enough to ensure profitability over the time horizon of this plan.

JOE'S BARBECUE
SUMMARY OF STRATEGIC PLAN, PAGE 2 OF 4
(1990–1999)

INTERNAL STRENGTHS AND WEAKNESSES

Strengths

Joe's has an experienced, stable base of dedicated employees. "Joe's Secret" barbecue sauce has a fanatic following and a regional reputation. Customers are mostly long-term regulars.

Weaknesses

The current facility is run-down. The lease will expire in 30 months. The company needs additional capital to expand. No strong second-string managers are available to take over any new sites. The company depends on only one raw meat supplier.

STRATEGIC DECISIONS MADE

1. **Base Location**

   Open a second restaurant in one of the new mall sites. Stop all capital spending on the present location and close it when road construction starts. Buy out of the old lease.

2. **Human Resources**

   Within eight months, hire a strong assistant manager for future expansion.

3. **Future Expansion**

   Purchase a catering truck to maintain the industrial-district customer base. Build catering business in the northwest part of the city, to expand to a second site within three years.

4. **Menu Revision**

   Add a salad bar. Change the kinds of meats prepared to those that customers are coming to favor. Change the portions and prices to accommodate older customers.

5. **Competition**

   Target Sam's Barbecue. Expand promotions using local print media, and reinforce with radio and TV. Exploit favorable restaurant reviews in the local press.

6. **New Business**

   Develop a mail-order business for "Joe's Secret" barbecue sauce.

7. **Secondary Supplier**

   Develop secondary suppliers, one per year for the next three years.

EXAMPLE (continued)

JOE'S BARBECUE
SUMMARY OF STRATEGIC PLAN, PAGE 3 OF 4
(1990–1999)

	(ADDITIONAL HISTORY)	1993 ACTUAL	1994 FORECAST	1995 PLAN	(ADDITIONAL PLAN)
INCOME STATEMENTS (000 OMITTED)					
SALES–DINING	(Insert additional	$270	$292	$313	(Insert additional
SALES–BARBEQUE SAUCE	columns in this	3	7	15	columns in this
COST OF SALES–DINING	range, one for	(149)	(161)	(172)	range, one for
COST OF SALES–BBQ SAUCE	each year of	(1)	(2)	(4)	each year of
GROSS MARGIN	ACTUAL historical	123	136	152	the future PLAN,
PAYROLL EXPENSE	results, usually	(68)	(73)	(78)	usually 5 years.)
FIXED AND ADMINISTRATIVE EXPENSE	the same as the	(12)	(15)	(16)	
OPERATING INCOME	number of future	43	48	58	
OTHER INCOME AND EXPENSE	years you are	(1)	(1)	(1)	
INTEREST EXPENSE	planning.)	(2)	(2)	(2)	
TAXES		(16)	(18)	(22)	
NET INCOME		$24	$27	$33	
BALANCE SHEETS (000 OMITTED)					
ASSETS					
CASH		$61	$82	$111	
OTHER CURRENT ASSETS		41	44	47	
TOTAL CURRENT ASSETS		102	126	158	
FIXED ASSETS (COST)		160	175	190	
CUMULATIVE DEPRECIATION		(93)	(108)	(124)	
NET FIXED ASSETS		67	67	66	
OTHER ASSETS		5	5	5	
TOTAL ASSETS		$174	$198	$229	
LIABILITIES					
CURRENT LIABILITIES		$23	$25	$28	
DEBT		25	20	15	
OTHER LIABILITIES		2	2	2	
OWNER EQUITY		124	151	184	
TOTAL LIABILITIES AND EQUITY		$174	$198	$229	

JOE'S BARBECUE
SUMMARY OF STRATEGIC PLAN, PAGE 4 OF 4
(1990 – 1999)

	(ADDITIONAL HISTORY)	1993 ACTUAL	1994 FORECAST	1995 PLAN	(ADDITIONAL PLAN)
CASH FLOW STATEMENTS (000 OMITTED)					
NET INCOME	(Insert additional	$24	$27	$33	(Insert additional
DEPRECIATION	columns in this	12	15	16	columns in this
NON CASH WORKING CAPITAL	range, one for	(2)	(1)	0	range, one for
CAPITAL SPENDING	each year of	(15)	(15)	(15)	each year of
CASH FROM OPERATIONS	ACTUAL historical	19	26	34	the future PLAN,
CHANGE IN DEBT	results, usually	(5)	(5)	(5)	usually 5 years.)
EQUITY INVESTMENTS	the same as the	0	0	0	
ALL OTHER	number of future	0	0	0	
NET CASH FLOW	years you are	14	21	29	
BEGINNING CASH	planning.)	47	61	82	
ENDING CASH		$61	$82	$111	
ECONOMICS AND BUSINESS INDICATORS					
ECONOMICS					
NUMBER OF ORDERS		14,300	14,700	15,000	
NUMBER OF CUSTOMERS		36,064	37,867	39,760	
MAIL ORDER BOTTLES OF SAUCE		500	1,000	2,000	
INDICATORS					
AVERAGE PRICE, $ PER ORDER		$18.90	$19.85	$20.84	
AVERAGE ORDER, $ PER CUSTOMER		$7.49	$7.71	$7.87	
AVERAGE CUSTOMERS PER ORDER		2.52	2.58	2.65	
AVERAGE PRICE, BOTTLE OF SAUCE		$6.95	$7.10	$7.35	

EXERCISES

Review the example. Identify the historical context, the discussion, the financials, the economics and the business indicators.

The historical context is _____

_____

_____

The discussion is _____

_____

_____

The financials are _____

_____

_____

The economics are _____

_____

_____

The business indicators are _____

_____

_____

Describe what your organization will look like five years from now.

_____

_____

_____

_____

_____

_____

_____

_____

SUMMARY OF PART 4

Strategic plans are broad projections which position the organization for long-term goals. Strategic plans should exist for the company as a whole, and also for each organization within it. To produce a strategic plan, create a mission statement, analyze the external environment, analyze the organization's internal capabilities, create a view of the future and build an inventory of strategic decisions. Document the plan with a description of the future, the financials, the economics and the business indicators.

P A R T

5

Annual Operating Plan Preliminaries

While strategic plans keep the organization oriented toward long-term goals, they are too general to serve as a good plan for the immediate future. So, at the end of each year, organizations build a detailed blueprint for the coming year: an annual operating plan. This is what most companies mean by a "budget."

The next few parts of this book show how to create an annual operating plan. You will discover that a surprising amount of planning work is *not* about lots of tiny numbers. It is about getting things done and making your organization more effective.

The examples in this book are for the usual, 12-month annual operating plan. Your company probably does things slightly differently. It may use a different fiscal year, or budget full-year totals and break them into monthly values later, etc. The tips and techniques that follow will work with any of these variations.

The annual operating plan process doesn't start with calculations, however. It starts with the major decisions described in this part.

DRAFTING ANNUAL GOALS

Before starting on the numbers, answer three questions about the coming year:

> *What must this organization do?* Make a list of the top priority things the organization must do next year. Keep it short—no more than ten items. Quit only when it is a good definition of a successful year.

> *Who will see that it gets done?* Fix personal responsibility for achieving the goals. (If you are a one-person organization, you already have a pretty good idea.)

> *When will it have to be finished?* Assign due dates.

LESS IS MORE

Most organizations try to do too many things. A list of one hundred ''priorities'' is misnamed. The organization will be leaner, more tightly focused, and more effective if you resist the urge to write down every bright idea you ever had. The list of annual goals should number no more than ten.

A PYRAMID OF GOALS

Assign each goal to someone who reports directly to you. Then have each of them break their goals into subgoals, for assignment to *their* subordinates. Repeat to the lowest level of the organization. The result is a pyramid of goals, all of which support the vital few of the organization as a whole. Your organization is focused; its tactical mission is clear. What's on that list gets done; what isn't, doesn't. Obviously, the list of goals must be internally consistent with one another.

Here is a sample list of goals:

1. Grow sales in existing regions 10% over last year with the same or improved profit margins.

2. Reduce cost of sales to 32% of sales.

3. Reduce total payroll expense to 35% of sales.

4. Ready 25 home office managers for promotion to director level.

5. Implement a new customer service network that cuts response time to four hours average, eight hours maximum.

6. Open a new branch office in Atlanta, which will break even by year end.

List the top three annual goals for your organization.

1. _____

_____

_____

2. _____

_____

_____

3. _____

_____

_____

ORGANIZATIONAL PLANNING

As annual goals are completed, a nagging question usually occurs: What must the organization look like to do this?

Probably something different.

Modern organizations are fluid. They shift people and responsibilities in order to meet new needs. To become something different, a company often needs a different organization. Are there underutilized people? Are they doing low-priority tasks? Are they stretched too thin? Do they need challenge, training or relief?

Annual goals and a firm idea of long-term direction provide a good starting point for reorganizing a firm.

Sketch out an effective, lean, focused organization. Build the plan that way. Realign departments, reassign individuals, create new functions, eliminate old ones. You are headed to the future. Create an organization that can get you there.

But don't be reckless. This is a highly leveraged activity. Done well, it yields astounding results. Done poorly, it is devastating. Few things good happen overnight. Be careful, and get appropriate expertise.

ORGANIZATION CHART

A REVISED ORGANIZATION CHART

Bent-Nail Builders, Inc., is changing the organization of its interior construction unit. They believe there is more profit in finishing interior surfaces than in doing major structural alterations. So they are repositioning the firm away from framing work and rough carpentry, and toward interior surface work. However, it is a more competitive business, so they are also adding a sales manager to assist the general manager in sales efforts.

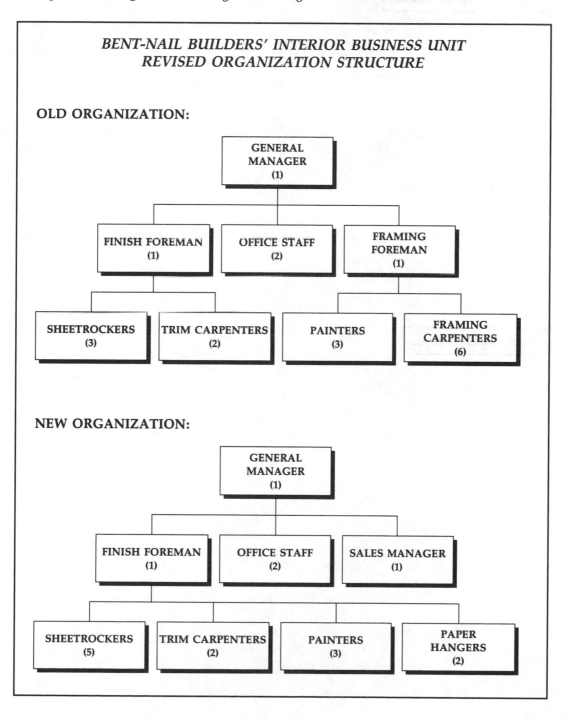

**BENT-NAIL BUILDERS' INTERIOR BUSINESS UNIT
REVISED ORGANIZATION STRUCTURE**

OLD ORGANIZATION:

- GENERAL MANAGER (1)
  - FINISH FOREMAN (1)
    - SHEETROCKERS (3)
    - TRIM CARPENTERS (2)
  - OFFICE STAFF (2)
  - FRAMING FOREMAN (1)
    - PAINTERS (3)
    - FRAMING CARPENTERS (6)

NEW ORGANIZATION:

- GENERAL MANAGER (1)
  - FINISH FOREMAN (1)
    - SHEETROCKERS (5)
    - TRIM CARPENTERS (2)
    - PAINTERS (3)
    - PAPER HANGERS (2)
  - OFFICE STAFF (2)
  - SALES MANAGER (1)

YOUR ORGANIZATION CHART

In the spaces below, draw (1) a summarized organization chart for your firm or department, and (2) a revised chart to meet the challenges of the future.

Existing organization:

New organization:

CREATING A FISCAL CALENDAR

Next, create a *fiscal calendar*.

Fiscal calendars are not normal calendars. Some retailers prefer a "year" of 13 four-week "months." Some manufacturers use a 4-4-5 calendar, where each quarter is composed of two "months" of 4 weeks each, followed by one of 5 weeks. Some retailers use a six-month "year," corresponding to merchandising seasons. Days at the end (or beginning) of each calendar month sometimes shift to make fiscal months the right size.

Fiscal calendars have many different kinds of days. In a month with 30 actual days, there might only be 20 business days (four weeks of 5 days each). If there were a paid holiday, there would be 20 payroll days, but 19 business days. If a manufacturing plant worked Saturdays, there would be 24 manufacturing days. If a retail store were open 7 days a week, there would be 28 sales days.

Locate or create fiscal calendars for each year to be planned, and one for each year of history to be analyzed. If necessary, design one appropriate to the needs of your business.

Fiscal calendars improve budget accuracy. For example, to plan salary expense using average "dollars per day," the correct calculation would be:

average payroll per day × *payroll days*

If someone slipped and used business days, they would understate labor expense in months that had holidays.

Fiscal calendars improve business knowledge. If a retail business shows a decline in sales versus the previous year, were things actually worse? Or was there a holiday that changed months? Or were there just fewer sales days? Sales per business day will answer the question.

JULY 1991						
S	M	T	W	T	F	S
	1	2	3	4	5	6
7	8	9	10	11	12	13
14	15	16	17	18	19	20
21	22	23	24	25	26	27
28	29	30	31			

EXAMPLE OF A FISCAL CALENDAR

In this fiscal calendar, there are 25 payroll days and 24 business days, since the 10th is a paid company holiday—the day the company was founded. Notice that the first 4 days of October have been added to fiscal September.

AMALGAMATED INDUSTRIES, INC.
FISCAL CALENDAR
SEPTEMBER 1991

SUNDAY	MONDAY	TUESDAY	WEDNESDAY	THURSDAY	FRIDAY	SATURDAY
1	2	3	4	5	6	7
8	9	10	11	12	13	14
15	16	17	18	19	20	21
22	23	24	25	26	27	28
29	30	1	2	3	4	5

What kind of fiscal calendar is your organization on?

_____

_____

How does it fit the needs of the business?

_____

_____

FISCAL MANAGERS

Who will build the plan and manage performance to achieve it? If you are responsible for a large organization, delegate those tasks to a group of *fiscal managers*. These are not new positions. "Fiscal manager" refers to an existing manager who is given formal budget responsibility.

A fiscal manager should be assigned to every income statement an organization generates. Twelve departments require 12 fiscal managers. Each has two responsibilities:

1. To build the plan.

2. To authorize expenses to be charged against it.

No one else can do either task—not even their superiors, not even someone in accounting with a "magic pen." (The only exception is an alternate when the fiscal manager is traveling.) At the total-company level, someone, probably the head finance person, should be the balance-sheet fiscal manager.

At the same time, review all procedures for authorizing payment. Be sure whoever writes checks has a written policy and a signature file to enforce who can approve charges and their authorization limits.

You have now fixed responsibility for achieving a plan in your organization.

(Although this can be an important part of control over unauthorized spending, it is obviously not a complete program. Be sure you have enough *other* controls in place to guard your organization's assets.)

Even if you are only responsible for a single department, be sure the rest of the organization knows there is only one fiscal manager for the department, and respects that fact.

> **PLANNER'S RULE #10**
> **WHATEVER HAPPENS, SOMEBODY IS RESPONSIBLE.**

Who fulfills the role of "fiscal manager" in your organization? Explain.

_____

_____

_____

ACCOUNTING SYSTEM TUNE-UP

Next, take a good look at the accounting system. It's kind of like a tree: when it's been around a while, it develops tangled branches and dead wood. Before planning, do some pruning.

Is the chart of accounts in good shape? Are sales detailed by accounts that easily track product lines? Are there separate cost-of-sales accounts to provide gross margin by product line? Are payroll and other expenses detailed enough to create a "mini income statement" for each product or service activity? Do the groupings of accounts make sense? Is the information *actionable* directly from the statements, without further analysis?

Does the hierarchy of cost and profit centers make sense? Most large organizations have a number of departments that roll up into summaries, and then, a consolidated income statement (or statement of expenses) is generated for each. Does this network of summary centers mirror the actual organization?

Is the system practical? Financial statements should be easily understandable to the lowest level that has to use them. Something is wrong if obvious questions always have complex answers or if only a handful of people can determine what is actually happening in the business. Statements should be action-oriented. If labor, for example, appears in cost of sales, operating expenses, administrative expenses, sales expenses, and other expenses, it will be hard to plan and manage human resources.

Can anyone else charge against your budget besides yourself?

_____

What changes do you think should be made?

_____

_____

Businesses with a lot of change accumulate a lot of deferred housekeeping. *Take care of it before creating your plan.*

PLANNER'S RULE #11:

ACCOUNTING EXISTS TO MAKE MANAGEMENT EASIER.

SUMMARY OF PART 5

Companies build an annual operating plan because the strategic plan is too general to be a good guide to short-term goals. However, before creating it, managers should handle preliminaries. They should draft a list of annual goals, defining the ''what, who, and when'' of success for the year. They should review the organization to see if reorganization is needed. They should draft a fiscal calendar to improve planning precision. Finally, fiscal managers should be assigned to each financial statement, and the accounting system should be tuned up for maximum usefulness.

P A R T

6

How to Budget Sales

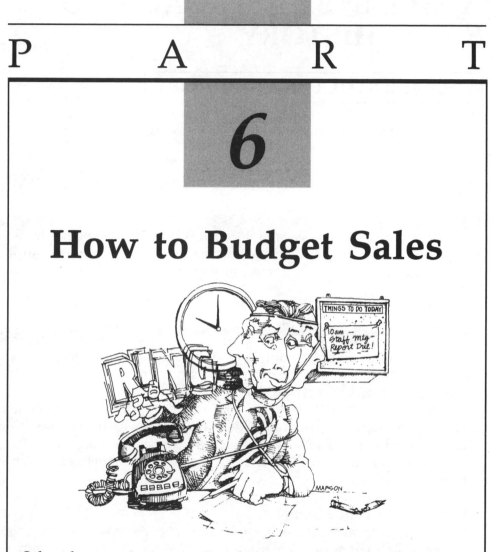

Sales plans are important. People may overlook expense problems, but bad sales plans cause businesses and careers to fail. They also mean inaccurate plans for expenses that are based on sales. For these reasons, sales accounts deserve serious planning effort.

Follow industry practices. Especially with sales plans, carefully research how the rest of the industry does it. Like local traffic laws, these practices vary widely, and it's dangerous to ignore them.

The next few pages deal with researching sales history, refining sales assumptions and building logical projections. At the end are several examples of sales plans.

A FIVE-STEP APPROACH TO SALES HISTORY

STEP 1: GATHER SALES HISTORY

Good sales plans require a good base of historical information.

- **How much?**
  Get at least the last full year; the previous five years are best.

- **How detailed?**
  Most companies group sales by lower levels of detail (geographical area, customer group, etc.). Rank this detailed information from the strongest to the weakest effect on sales, and put your research and analysis against the most important.

- **Don't forget the economics.**
  Even though most sales information is in dollars, try to get corresponding information in *units sold* (pounds of soybeans, hours of service, etc.).

- **Disaggregate or summarized data?**
  When building separate budgets for a number of locations, customers or product lines, it is best to get detailed data for each one—say on a computer diskette, *if you have the skill and software to manipulate it.* Otherwise, summarized data is best. The key is adequate access at the level of detail needed.

- **What if there is no history?**
  Some firms are start-ups, or have bad internal records. The only choice is to research the market from external sources. What did similar companies do? What are the most important sales factors?

- **Check performance requirements.**
  Review the strategic plan. What must this year do in sales? What are the expectations of the bank, the investors, your superiors?

STEP 2: NORMALIZE SALES HISTORY

Never use raw history as a basis for planning any account, especially sales. What happened in previous years that was unusual? Examples include unusual weather, labor strikes, supplier problems, street construction, etc. Even advertising campaigns might have to be normalized. Back the effect of such events out of both dollar and unit histories *before using them to plan the future.*

Describe three unusual events that should be backed out of your business's sales history to normalize it.

_____

_____

_____

STEP 3: ADJUST FOR SEASONALITY

Most company's sales vary with the time of year. Understand this seasonal variation, or seasonality of sales. Retailers do more business in December, motels do more business in summer, landscape businesses do more business in spring, etc. The calculation example at the end of this part shows one approach to adjusting plans for seasonality.

Describe the seasonal nature of sales in your own business. When do sales peak?

_____

When is the slow season?

_____

How variable is the seasonality of sales in your firm?

_____

A FIVE-STEP APPROACH TO
SALES HISTORY (continued)

STEP 4: ADJUST PLANS FOR MATURITY

New businesses have weak sales followed by rapid growth. Later, sales are strong and growth falls off—the business (or the particular location) is *mature*. The process may take several years. Know where a business is on the maturity curve. If you are planning many sites, group them by age, and plan accordingly.

Does maturity play a role in sales calculations for your business?

_____

How long does it take a typical store, sales office or production facility to stop losing money?

_____

To reach its full sales and profit potential?

_____

Is it usually a fast start and slow finish, or vice versa?

_____

STEP 5: ANALYZE UNIT PRICE

"Unit" information gives insight into average price. What does the history say about price behavior? Develop a deliberate pricing policy. If average price is decaying, can revenue be made up through volume? If unit price is increasing, can even more revenue be gained by increasing the price further? Decreasing it to gain a larger market? Where possible, plan sales in both units and average price, after carefully analyzing the relationship between them.

ASSUMPTIONS: IMPROVING YOUR VISION OF THE FUTURE

After analyzing historical data, make sound assumptions about the future.

▶ **Qualitative is not (necessarily) bad.** There are lots of numbers available for past performance, but precious few about the future. A lot of assumptions about the future must be "soft," verbal assessments. To the extent possible, translate them into hard, numerical assumptions.

▶ **Listen to customers and competitors.** If possible, contact them directly. Survey the sales force. What are their projections? What are their expansion plans?

▶ **Research the environment.** What is available about society, culture, government and other external things that affect your business? Do industry, trade or general business publications have useful information?

▶ **Research your market.** Companies that dominate their industry will be concerned about industry growth, market share, etc. Local businesses may be more concerned about the town's largest employer. Focus on the particulars of your firm.

List the five most important external factors that influence sales in your business. What is the best source of information for analyzing each?

External Factors that Influence Sales	**Best Source of Information**
1. _____	_____
2. _____	_____
3. _____	_____
4. _____	_____
5. _____	_____

PROJECTIONS: BUILDING A CHAIN OF INFERENCE

An annual operating plan can force a business to look at sales in a disciplined way. Basically this means listing the major factors which influence sales, and assessing their probable impact, to project next year's sales. Here are some examples:

MARKET SHARE—Company A is a national market power. The industry projections are for national growth of 8%. The company intends to gain an additional 2% from new products, and 2% more from competitors. Total growth expected: 12% over the previous year.

LOCAL ECONOMY—Company B is a local service company. The city planning commission projects population growth next year at 4%. The company also expects 10% additional sales from a new location, and a further 10% from two new services. Total growth expected: 24% over the previous year.

COMMODITY PRICING—Company C is an old firm in a mature industry. Most competition is based on price. Interviews with customers indicate they will buy 10% more product next year, but prices will be 10% lower due to increased competition. Total growth expected: 0% over the previous year.

In the space below, describe your preferred sales projection philosophy. List another possibility. What are the advantages and disadvantages of each?

My preferred philosophy is: _____

Its advantages are: _____

_____

Its disadvantages are: _____

_____

Another possibility: _____

_____

Advantages: _____

Disadvantages: _____

> **PLANNER'S RULE #12:**
>
> **EVERY PROJECTION FOR EVERY ACCOUNT MUST HAVE A CLEAR RATIONALE.**

EXAMPLE OF SALES BUDGET FROM MARKET SHARE

For firms with a commanding national presence, a sales planning philosophy based on market share could make most sense. Here is a projection that might be used in a strategic plan.

FLIPPO'S FUZZY DICE IMPORTERS, INC.
SALES PLAN
1993–1995

	1993	1994	1995
1. CALCULATE NATIONAL MARKET SIZE.			
(a) BEGINNING NATIONAL MARKET SIZE (units)	100,000	105,000	110,250
(b) EXPECTED GROWTH IN MARKET + 100%	105%	105%	105%
(c) EXPECTED MARKET SIZE (a times b)	105,000	110,250	115,763
2. CALCULATE COMPANY MARKET SHARE.			
(d) MARKET SHARE (units)	15%	17%	19%
(e) EXPECTED CHANGE IN MARKET SHARE	2%	2%	2%
(f) EXPECTED MARKET SHARE	17%	19%	21%
3. CALCULATE COMPANY SALES.			
(g) NATIONAL MARKET SIZE (units, c)	105,000	110,250	115,763
(h) EXPECTED MARKET SHARE (f)	17%	19%	21%
(i) EXPECTED COMPANY SALES (units, g times h)	17,850	20,948	24,310
4. ADJUST FOR PRICE CHANGES.			
(j) SALES (units, i)	17,850	20,948	24,310
(k) UNIT PRICE (dollars, expected to increase 3% per year)	$5.00	$5.15	$5.30
SALES PLAN (dollars, j times k)	**$89,250**	**$107,882**	**$128,843**

However, you don't have to be a national power to use this approach. Rightnow Office Services, Inc., only serves clients in a single large office complex.

RIGHTNOW OFFICE SERVICES, INC.
SALES PLAN
1993–1995

	1993	1994	1995
(a) MAXIMUM TENANTS IN THIS BUILDING	125	125	125
(b) EMPTY OFFICE SUITES	50	40	30
(c) FILLED OFFICES	75	85	95
(d) EXPECTED MARKET SHARE	30%	32%	34%
(e) EXPECTED NUMBER OF CLIENTS	23	27	32
(f) SALES PER CLIENT (dollars, expected to grow 5% per year)	$7,000	$7,350	$7,718
PLANNED SALES (dollars)	**$161,000**	**$198,450**	**$246,976**

EXAMPLE OF A SALES BUDGET FROM HISTORY

This approach doesn't require unit information; using units would be better, but such data aren't always available.

SAM'S FAMOUS (BETTER'N JOE'S) BARBECUE
SALES PLAN
1993

1. CALCULATE SEASONAL RATIOS.

	JAN	FEB	MAR	(OTHER MONTHS)	YEAR
(a) REPORTED SALES (dollars, previous year)	$31,094	$16,094	$27,940	(Insert figures for	$340,000
(b) BACK OUT UNUSUAL OR ONE–TIME EVENTS:				other	
• CONVENTION BUSINESS	($5,000)			months in	($5,000)
• ROAD CONSTRUCTION		$10,000		this range.)	$10,000
• MINOR FIRE			$5,000		$5,000
(c) NORMALIZED SALES (a+b)	$26,094	$26,094	$32,940		$350,000
(d) PRICE INCREASE	100%	102%	102%		
(e) DEFLATED SALES (c/d)	$26,094	$25,582	$32,294		$343,650
(f) BUSINESS DAYS (old year)	28	28	35		364
(g) SALES PER BUSINESS DAY (e/f)	$932	$914	$923		$944
(h) FULL–YEAR AVERAGE SALES PER DAY (g, last col.)	$944	$944	$944		$944
(i) SEASONAL RATIO (g/h)	98.7%	96.8%	97.8%		100.0%

2. CALCULATE EXPECTED GROWTH IN BASE BUSINESS.

	FULL YEAR
(j) LAST YEAR AVERAGE SALES PER DAY (h)	$944
(k) PLANNED "REAL" SALES GROWTH	105%
(l) PLANNED SALES PER DAY (j times k)	$991

3. REVERSE THE PROCESS.

	JAN	FEB	MAR	(OTHER MONTHS)	YEAR
(m) PLANNED SALES PER DAY (l)	$991	$991	$991		
(n) SEASONAL RATIO (i)	98.7%	96.8%	97.8%		
(o) PLANNED SALES PER DAY (m times n)	$978	$959	$969		
(p) PLANNED PRICE INCREASE (100% = none)	100%	100%	102%		
(q) SALES PER DAY AFTER PRICE INCREASE (o times p)	$978	$959	$988		
(r) BUSINESS DAYS (new year)	28	28	35		364
(s) NORMAL SALES (q times r)	$27,384	$26,852	$34,580		$367,948
(t) ADJUST FOR EXTRAORDINARY EVENTS:					
• CONVENTION #1	$5,000				$5,000
• CONVENTION #2		$4,000			$4,000
• VACATION			($3,000)		($3,000)
(u) **PLANNED SALES, (s+t)**	**$32,384**	**$30,852**	**$31,580**		**$373,948**

SALES BUDGET FROM HISTORY (continued)

Sam has decided to plan at a lower level of detail than total sales. While it would be possible to repeat the previous process for each sales category, Sam doesn't think the proportion of sales generated by each sales category will change. Therefore, Sam built his detail plans by allocating total sales to detailed sales accounts, on the basis of history.

SAM'S FAMOUS (BETTER'N JOE'S) BARBECUE
SALES PLAN
1993

1. RESEARCH HISTORY (sales dollars).

	LAST YEAR	
(a) BEVERAGE SERVICE	$34,000	(Under what circumstances would it make sense for Sam to analyze the percent of sales by product line by month?)
(b) FOOD SERVICE	153,000	
(c) SPECIAL ORDERS	85,000	
(d) BARBECUE SAUCE	51,000	
(e) ALL OTHER SALES	17,000	
(f) TOTAL SALES	$340,000	

2. CALCULATE PERCENTAGE OF TOTAL SALES.

	LAST YEAR
(g) BEVERAGE SERVICE (a/f)	10%
(h) FOOD SERVICE (b/f)	45%
(i) SPECIAL ORDERS (c/f)	25%
(j) BARBECUE SAUCE (d/f)	15%
(k) ALL OTHER SALES (e/f)	5%
(l) TOTAL SALES (f/f)	100%

3. MULTIPLY PERCENTAGES TIMES TOTAL SALES PLAN FOR THE MONTH.

	JAN	FEB	MAR	(OTHER MONTHS)	FULL YEAR
(m) TOTAL SALES PLAN (from previous chart)	$32,384	$30,852	$31,580	(Insert figures for other months in this range.)	$373,948
(n) *DETAIL SALES PLANS:*					
• *BEVERAGE SERVICE, ACCT #1001 (m times g)*	*$3,238*	*$3,085*	*$3,158*		*$37,395*
• *FOOD SERVICE, ACCT # 1002 (m times h)*	*14,573*	*13,883*	*14,211*		*$168,277*
• *SPECIAL ORDERS, ACCT # 1003 (m times i)*	*8,096*	*7,713*	*7,895*		*$93,488*
• *BARBECUE SAUCE, ACCT # 1004 (m times j)*	*4,858*	*4,628*	*4,737*		*$56,093*
• *ALL OTHER SALES, ACCT # 1005 (m times k)*	*1,619*	*1,543*	*1,579*		*$18,695*
(o) TOTAL SALES (total of items in "n")	$32,384	$30,852	$31,580		$373,948

SUMMARY OF PART 6

Sales plans are more important than expense plans. Each industry has its own standard way to project sales, which can serve as a model for your firm. History is important, but should always be normalized before projecting sales or any other account. Understand the seasonality of sales in your business. Sales plans should be adjusted for the maturity of the business. Develop a specific sales projection philosophy.

P A R T

7

How to Budget Cost of Sales

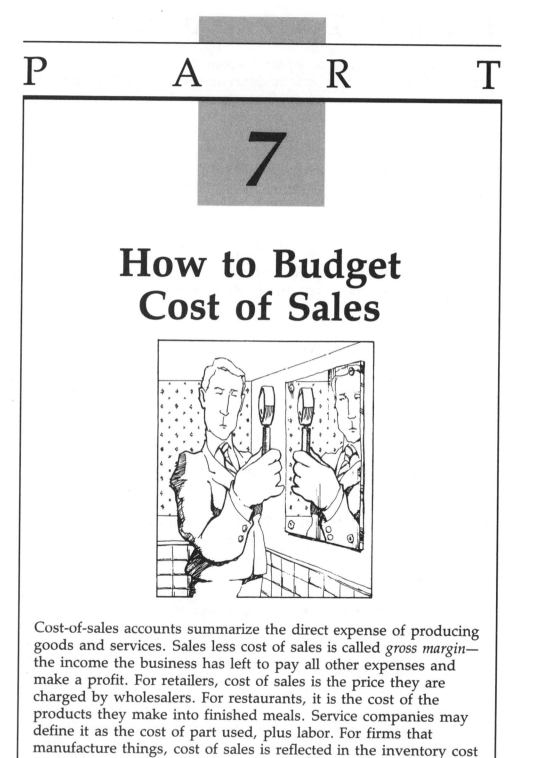

Cost-of-sales accounts summarize the direct expense of producing goods and services. Sales less cost of sales is called *gross margin*—the income the business has left to pay all other expenses and make a profit. For retailers, cost of sales is the price they are charged by wholesalers. For restaurants, it is the cost of the products they make into finished meals. Service companies may define it as the cost of part used, plus labor. For firms that manufacture things, cost of sales is reflected in the inventory cost of an item, which in turn reflects the cost of the entire plant that produced it (labor, overhead, utilities, parts, raw materials, etc.).

DIFFERENT APPROACHES

Like sales plans, cost-of-sales plans depend a great deal on the specific business. The best advice is to understand how it is calculated in the particular organization, and duplicate that calculation to the extent possible. Here is an overview of some strategies:

▶ **MARGINS.** If the business has stable margins, cost of sales can be forecast as a simple percentage of sales. For example, if cost of sales has run 33% of sales for the past five years, it will probably run 33% of sales in the future (adjusted for any price increases).

▶ **SUPPLIER QUOTES.** If the cost of sales is based on a few key suppliers, quotes and contracts may supply the needed information.

▶ **STANDARD COSTS.** Manufacturing businesses that use standard costs really only have two choices:

1. Use some kind of high-level assumptions based on history.

2. Execute a complete budget process for the manufacturing plant.

Such companies usually have people responsible for standard costing, and planners usually can turn to them.

▶ **ANALYTICAL APPROACH.** Some businesses find it makes most sense to tear cost of sales apart; analyze each part in terms of data, assumptions and projections; and then combine the result into a total number. An example: raw materials are 10%, supplier parts are 85% and labor is 5% of cost of sales. These costs will change by 3%, 10% and 5%, respectively. Therefore, cost of sales will increase approximately 9%:

$$(3\% \text{ of } 10\%) + (10\% \text{ of } 85\%) + (5\% \text{ of } 5\%)$$
$$= \quad 0.3\% + 8.5\% + 0.25\%$$
$$= \quad 9.05\%$$

A more detailed example of the analytical approach is shown on the facing page.

EXAMPLE OF AN ANALYTICAL APPROACH

For simplicity, this example assumes that Granny builds and sells her inventory in the same month. In reality, most firms would keep these production costs on their balance sheet as INVENTORY, and then recognize them as COST OF SALES whenever the goods were sold.

GRANNY'S HEIRLOOM STORAGE CHEST COMPANY
COST OF SALES PLAN
1993

	JAN	FEB	MAR	(OTHER MONTHS)	FULL YEAR
1. RESEARCH LAST YEAR'S HISTORY.					
FINANCIAL HISTORY					
(a) COST OF HARDWARE, ACCT # 2001	$5,000	$10,000	$20,000	(Insert	$405,000
(b) COST OF PRODUCTION LABOR, ACCT # 2002	17,500	35,000	70,000	figures for	1,417,500
(c) COST OF WOOD, ACCT # 2003	12,000	24,000	48,000	other	972,000
(d) PACKAGING EXPENSE, ACCT # 2003	1,000	2,000	4,000	months	81,000
(e) PRODUCTION OVERHEAD, ACCT # 2004	7,000	7,000	8,750	here.)	91,000
TOTAL	$42,500	$78,000	$150,750		$2,966,500
ECONOMIC HISTORY					
(f) NUMBER OF STORAGE CHESTS SOLD	100	200	400		8,100
(g) BOARD FEET OF WOOD USED	6,000	12,000	24,000		486,000
(h) HOURS OF PRODUCTION LABOR	2,500	5,000	10,000		202,500
(i) BUSINESS DAYS	28	28	35		364
BUSINESS INDICATOR HISTORY					
(j) HOURS OF LABOR PER CHEST (h/f)	25.0	25.0	25.0		
(k) LABOR RATE (dollars/hour) (b/h)	$7.00	$7.00	$7.00		
(l) BOARD FEET OF WOOD PER CHEST (g/f)	60	60	60		
(m) COST OF WOOD PER BOARD FOOT (c/g)	$2.00	$2.00	$2.00		
(n) HARDWARE COST PER CHEST (a/f)	$50.00	$50.00	$50.00		
(o) PACKAGING COST PER CHEST (d/f)	$10.00	$10.00	$10.00		
(p) OVERHEAD $ PER BUSINESS DAY (e/i)	$250.00	$250.00	$250.00		

ANALYTICAL APPROACH (continued)

	JAN	FEB	MAR	(OTHER MONTHS)	YEAR

2. ESTIMATE THE FUTURE VALUES OF BUSINESS INDICATORS.

The company sees no change in productivity; it will take the same number of hours. We plan to give plant employees a 5% raise, so labor rates will increase that much. Better use of scrap will allow the amount of wood to decrease from 60 to 55 board feet per chest. The cost of wood per board foot is expected to remain the same as last year. We also plan on a large increase in hardware prices, based on a quotation from our suppliers. Overhead will go up 3% due to supervisory salaries. Suppliers quote packaging at the same price as last year.

BUSINESS INDICATOR PLAN					
(q) HOURS OF LABOR PER CHEST (j)	25.0	25.0	25.0	(Insert	
(r) LABOR RATE (dollars/hour, k times 1.05)	$7.35	$7.35	$7.35	figures for	
(s) BOARD FEET OF WOOD PER CHEST (line l reduced by 5)	55	55	55	other	
(t) COST OF WOOD PER BOARD FOOT (supplier quote)	$2.00	$2.00	$2.00	months	
(u) HARDWARE COST PER CHEST (supplier quote)	$63.00	$63.00	$63.00	here.)	
(v) PACKAGING COST PER CHEST (supplier quote)	$10.00	$10.00	$10.00		
(w) OVERHEAD $ PER BUSINESS DAY (line o times 1.03)	$258.00	$258.00	$258.00		

3. FORECAST/CALCULATE THE ECONOMICS.

The number of chests to be sold has already been planned, in the sales plan. Business days are known. The other economic measures are simple calculations.

ECONOMIC PLAN					
(x) NUMBER OF CHESTS TO BE SOLD (sales plan)	110	220	440		8,910
(y) BOARD FEET OF WOOD USED (s times x)	6,050	12,100	24,200		490,050
(z) HOURS OF PRODUCTION LABOR (q times x)	2,750	5,500	11,000		222,750
(aa) BUSINESS DAYS (as planned)	28	28	35		364

4. CALCULATE THE FINANCIAL PLAN.

FINANCIAL PLAN					
COST OF HARDWARE, ACCT # 2001 (u times x)	$6,930	$13,860	$27,720		$561,330
COST OF PRODUCTION LABOR, ACCT # 2002 (r times z)	20,213	40,425	80,850		1,637,215
COST OF WOOD, ACCT#2003 (s times t times x)	12,100	24,200	48,400		980,100
COST OF PACKAGING, ACCT # 2003 (v times x)	1,100	2,200	4,400		89,100
PRODUCTION OVERHEAD, ACCT # 2004 (w times aa)	7,224	7,224	9,030		93,912
TOTAL COST OF SALES (OR INCREASE IN INVENTORY)	$47,567	$87,909	$170,400		$3,361,657

List the components of cost of sales in your company—the equivalents of items a–e in the Granny's Heirloom budget.

_____

_____

_____

_____

_____

_____

Which cost-of-sales forecast strategy makes the most sense for your firm?

_____

_____

What means are available for you to anticipate increases in cost of sales?

_____

_____

_____

_____

_____

_____

_____

_____

SUMMARY OF PART 7

"Cost of sales" refers to expense accounts that capture the cost of goods or services. Since practices vary widely, it is important to understand exactly how the cost is calculated in each particular firm. Strategies for producing cost-of-sales plans include percent of sales, supplier quotes, standard costs and the analytical approach.

8

How to Budget Labor Expense

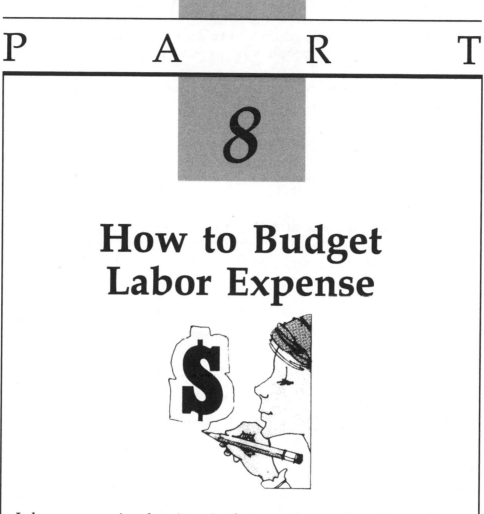

Labor expense is a key item in the annual operating plan. Why? Because:

- Payroll is often the largest *controllable* expense.

- Many other expenses are strongly influenced by headcount.

- It is *highly leveraged.* If a business buys too few pencils, life goes on. But human-resource errors are an efficient way to kill any enterprise.

- Ethics. Labor plans affect careers and lifestyles.

Total labor expense can be hard to find, since it pops up in many different places. It may be in cost of sales, sales expense, administrative expense or its own separate category. The good planner sniffs out all these places, and budgets accordingly.

POLICY BEFORE PLANNING

Planning provides an opportunity to reflect on the organization, its culture, and how to manage the people who work there.

There are many issues. Should the organization reward teamwork or individuals? Should it encourage turnover or longevity? Should it give everyone an increase, or only "stars"? Should incentive programs be based on company performance, or individual contribution? Should cost-of-living increases be given on the individual anniversaries, or all at the same time? Should there be frequent promotions and few increases in grade, or vice versa? The list goes on and on.

Each such decision has a different impact on productivity and the firm's ultimate success. Yet the cost might be the same. Planning is the ideal opportunity to address these issues, and turn the organization toward its strategic goals.

Proceed carefully. As with all important decisions, bad decisions can have devastating effects.

> **PLANNER'S RULE #13:**
> **POLICY ALWAYS PRECEDES PLANNING.**

APPROPRIATE LEVELS OF DETAIL

There are many strategies for planning payroll expenses.

- At the finest level of detail, a labor plan can be created by doing proforma payroll calculations for each person for each month for the next year.

- At the most summarized level, a labor plan is last year's results, plus a certain percentage increase.

- In between are a variety of methods, such as planning by position, average cost and average number of employees in that position.

The planning tools available determine which method to use. Some firms have tools to calculate a payroll plan, by month, for everyone in the company, and summarize the results. Other firms with no such tools and several thousand employees, must use a summary method.

Is payroll expense a major or minor item in your firm's budget?

_____

Is it the largest controllable expense?

_____

How many different places in your income statement include some form of payroll expenses?

_____

_____

What are the advantages of that approach? Explain.

_____

_____

_____

_____

PAYROLL CALCULATIONS

Regardless of method, to build a payroll plan, first calculate base compensation, then calculate taxes and benefits.

BASE COMPENSATION

Employees are either exempt or nonexempt as defined by the Fair Labor Standards Act.

- *Exempt (Salaried) Employees.* Base compensation for these individuals is their monthly salary. (However, some firms have overtime provisions even for exempt employees.)

- *Nonexempt (Hourly) Employees.* Base compensation for these individuals is the total number of normal hours worked, multiplied by the hourly rate; plus the number of overtime hours worked, multiplied by 1.5 times the hourly rate. "Normal" hours usually means 40 hours per week, but there are exceptions. (This assumes a typical overtime wage rate of 150% of normal rates.)

TAXES

Employers are required to pay taxes on payroll expense, beyond those they collect from employees. These vary from state to state, from city to city, and from year to year. Most include:

- *Social Security (F.I.C.A.).* Employers must pay a certain percentage of each employee's wages, up to a specific ceiling, into the social security fund. (1991 rates: 6.2% on the first $53,400 + 1.45% on the first $125,000.)

- *Federal Unemployment Tax.* Employers must pay a percentage of employee compensation into the federal unemployment insurance fund (1991 rates: 6.2% on the first $7,000, less a credit up to 5.4% for payment of state unemployment tax.)

- *State Unemployment Tax.* Similar to the federal tax, but it varies from state to state, and with the number of claims, etc.

- *Others.* There may be other payroll taxes for your particular area; taxes and rates change with each legislative session. Be sure you know all the relevant taxes and current rates for your firm.

Talk to whoever does payroll taxes for your organization. What payroll taxes apply where you do business? What are the current rates?

_____

_____

_____

_____

_____

_____

BENEFITS

There are thousands of different ways to plan and account for benefits. Your firm may charge individual departments; it may create a standard benefits charge; it may charge each employee; or it may do something entirely different. Understand how benefits are charged, and build your plan accordingly.

How are benefits charged in your organization?

_____

What expenses are included?

_____

_____

What steps should be taken to estimate those costs for next year?

_____

_____

_____

_____

HANDLING INCREASES

There are at least four different means of adjusting wages and salaries:

► **COST OF LIVING.** Most firms adjust all wages and salaries from time to time, to compensate for creeping inflation, and to stay competitive with other firms.

► **MERIT.** An increase may be given to an individual for outstanding performance.

► **PROMOTION.** An increase is usually given to an individual when he or she is given increased responsibilities.

► **SENIORITY.** An increase may be given to an individual for length of service.

Your salary plan should reflect policy on each issue.

How does your firm handle payroll increases?

_____

_____

What are the advantages of this approach?

_____

_____

The disadvantages?

_____

_____

How could it be changed to make planning easier?

_____

_____

It is also important to maintain *position control*. Individuals should be rewarded only in the context of planned positions.

Put another way, the planning process has determined that a certain network of positions is necessary for company success. Regardless of individual performance, that position still has a maximum value to the firm. Beyond that, the outstanding employee must reach for the next higher position. Successful companies plan and manage a network of positions, while they encourage employees to achieve personal and career success *within that network*.

How does your organization maintain position control?

_____

_____

PLANNER'S RULE #14:

PLAN POSITIONS, NOT PEOPLE.

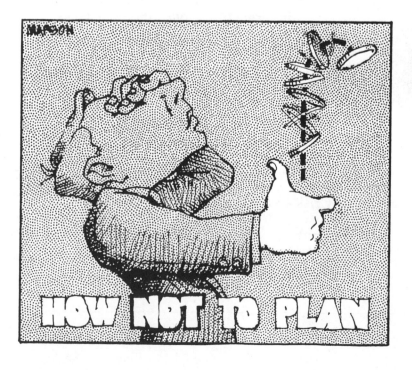

LABOR PLANNING TIPS

VACANCY. No company is totally staffed all the time. When people leave, it takes time to fill the vacancy. Therefore, in organizations with several hundred people, it may be possible to reduce planned payroll by several percentage points.

PAYROLL OVERHEAD. Slogging through taxes, benefits, and other *payroll overhead* takes a lot of time. Here's a shortcut. Calculate total payroll overhead, then divide it by the total wages and salaries, excluding taxes, benefits, etc. This will give you a *payroll overhead percentage.* Charge each department for wages, salaries and overtime, plus this payroll overhead percentage. Throw the proceeds into a single department, and pay all such charges from that department.

NEW HIRES. Headcount additions must be carefully monitored. Make beginning, ending and average headcount an *accountable* number. Force a justification of each new employee individually.

TEMPORARIES AND CONSULTANTS. Sometimes companies reduce payroll budgets, but the savings never occur—they just move to part-time employees, temporary help, and consultants. Smart companies plan and evaluate these expenses in terms of *equivalent full-time heads*.

How does your firm control temporary help, consultants and part-time positions?

_____

_____

_____

Does this present any risk to controlling labor?

_____

_____

_____

_____

EXAMPLE OF A LABOR BUDGET

Companies with few employees, or large companies with good tools, can create the payroll budget by almost duplicating the exact calculations for every employee for every month in the coming year. Here is an example of those kinds of calculations. Remember, these are only examples. Check with your professionals to verify the complete list of taxes and current rates. In this example, corporate policy charges each department 10% of base wages and salary for benefits. Your company probably does something different, so duplicate that calculation. Do not forget wage and salary adjustments, new hires, reductions in force, etc.

POSITION: MANAGER					
CURRENTLY FILLED BY: SUSAN SMITH CLASSIFICATION: EXEMPT (SALARIED)	JAN	FEB	MAR	(OTHER MONTHS)	TOTAL
MONTHLY SALARY	$6,000	$6,000	$6,000	(Insert	$73,500
FICA	459	459	459	figures for	4,377
FUTA	48	8	0	other	56
SUTA	324	54	0	months in	378
BENEFITS	600	600	600	this range.)	7,350
PAYROLL BUDGET, SUSAN	$7,431	$7,121	$7,059		$85,661

POSITION: EXECUTIVE ASSISTANT					
CURRENTLY FILLED BY: CORRINNE ALEXANDER CLASSIFICATION: NONEXEMPT (HOURLY)	JAN	FEB	MAR	(OTHER MONTHS)	TOTAL
NORMAL EARNINGS					
NORMAL WAGE RATE PER HOUR	$7.35	$7.35	$7.35		
NORMAL HOURS WORKED	160	160	200		2,080
NORMAL EARNINGS	$1,176	$1,176	$1,470		$16,302
OVERTIME EARNINGS					
ANNUAL CONVENTION	0	10	0		20
YEAR–END REPORTS	20	0	0		40
TOTAL OVERTIME HOURS	20	10	0		60
OVERTIME WAGE RATE PER HOUR	$11.03	$11.03	$11.03		
OVERTIME EARNINGS	$221	$110	$0		$691
TOTAL EARNINGS					
NORMAL + OVERTIME EARNINGS	$1,397	$1,286	$1,470		$16,993
FICA	107	98	112		1,299
FUTA	11	10	12		55
SUTA	75	69	79		376
BENEFITS	140	129	147		1,700
PAYROLL BUDGET, CORRINE	$1,730	$1,592	$1,820		$20,423

EXAMPLE OF A LABOR BUDGET (continued)

When you are faced with a tight deadline, too many employees, or inadequate tools, it is sometimes necessary to do a quick estimate of the labor budget. Here is one method. Taxes are estimated proportionally to last year. Notice that the key figures are year end, not the average figures for the full year, because the future year starts where the old year leaves off. Fractional people are parttime employees, fulltime employees hired for less than a full year, etc. (Be careful with averages. If everyone receives a 6% increase halfway through the year, the average is only 3% for the year.)

TOMMY'S MACHINE SHOP
PAYROLL PLAN ESTIMATE
1993

	YEAR END	RAISES	NEXT YEAR	NEW HIRES	TOTAL
(a) NUMBER OF EMPLOYEES					
ADMINISTRATION	4.0		4.0	0.5	4.5
SALES	5.0		5.0	1.5	6.5
PRODUCTION	18.0		18.0	6.5	24.5
TOTAL	27.0		27.0	8.5	35.5

	YEAR END	RAISES	NEXT YEAR	NEW HIRES	TOTAL
(b) AVERAGE SALARY					
ADMINISTRATION	$32,273	103%	$33,241	$25,000	
SALES	$38,619	102%	$39,391	$30,000	
PRODUCTION	$27,241	107%	$29,148	$22,000	

	YEAR END	RAISES	NEXT YEAR	NEW HIRES	TOTAL
(c) TOTAL PAYROLL BUDGET (a times b)					
ADMINISTRATION			$132,964	$12,500	$145,464
SALES			196,955	45,000	241,955
PRODUCTION			524,664	143,000	667,664
SUBTOTAL			854,583	200,500	1,055,083
TAXES:					
FICA			65,373	15,338	80,711
FUTA			1,880	441	2,321
SUTA			9,778	2,294	12,072
BENEFITS			256,375	60,150	316,525
TOTAL			$1,187,989	$278,723	$1,466,712

SUMMARY OF PART 8

Labor expense is important because it is usually the largest controllable expense. Plan it by position, not by individual. Labor policy should be set before any calculations are done. Calculation strategies are determined by the tools available. Different calculations are needed for exempt and nonexempt employees. The fundamental calculation is:

base compensation + taxes + benefits = payroll expense

Taxes include FICA, FUTA, SUTA, and possibly others, depending on location. Payroll adjustments can be viewed as either cost-of-living allowances, merit increases, promotions or seniority increases. Large organizations can usually reduce payroll budgets a bit, due to the usual number of open positions. A standard payroll overhead percentage can simplify labor planning. New positions must be thoroughly scrutinized. Part-timers, temporaries and consultants must be planned as full-time-equivalent heads.

P A R T

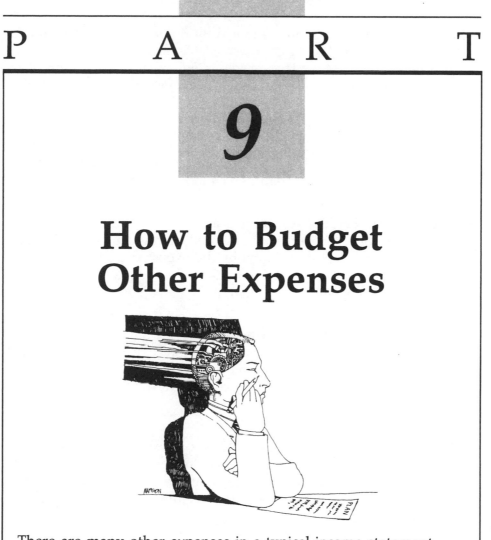

9

How to Budget Other Expenses

There are many other expenses in a typical income statement. They may be called overhead, operating, or perhaps general and administrative expenses.

The key to planning these expenses is to realize that most of them are a function of something else which is known. Analyze history and try to uncover these relationships. Here are some suggestions on these expenses, followed by examples of calculations.

PLANNER'S RULE #15:

ANYTHING THAT ISN'T KNOWN DEPENDS ON SOMETHING THAT IS.

TYPICAL APPROACHES

TRAVEL EXPENSES. Decide who can fly first class, who can stay in luxury hotels, what kind of rental car is acceptable, etc. Define it by level of employee, and publish the policy. That makes travel expense a function of the number of trips, the length of stay and what level of employee is traveling.

EXPENSES RELATED TO SALES. Many expenses are related to sales. This includes obvious things like sales commissions; but freight, returns and allowances, and packaging might also be good candidates. If a particular account always runs a certain percentage of sales, then forecast it that way.

SEASONAL EXPENSES. Are there seasonal trends in some accounts? Natural gas, heating oil, and electricity are good candidates. The calculation is simple: multiply last year's total by the expected price change, then respread that total across the months of the coming year, in the same proportion as last year.

EXPENSES RELATED TO BUSINESS DAYS. Some expenses are a function of the number of business days in the month such as a store manager's overnight report, dispatched each business day. Some accounting departments also allocate rent, interest, etc., according to the number of business days in the month.

IRREGULAR EXPENSES. Other expenses are simply irregular. Things like property taxes, business licenses, insurance payments, etc., may hit only one or two months of the year. Look at the year-end income statement, identify likely candidates, then scan monthly statements to see when they occur.

EXPENSES RELATED TO HEADCOUNT. Many expenses are related to headcount. Telephone, travel and office supplies are likely candidates. Those who are managing a budget process may want to publish approved guidelines for office supplies, etc., based on a set number of dollars per person per month.

SCHEDULED EXPENSES. Depreciation, rent payments, etc., are examples of *scheduled expenses*. The only basis is a written schedule, somewhere, that details the amount. Locate the schedule. Interest, depreciation, rent and amortization expenses are other candidates.

TAX AND INTEREST. Most businesses have a simple percentage that reflects the consolidated tax rate on the business, which they use for planning purposes. *This may not be accurate enough.* Check with finance professionals about the specifics of tax, interest, etc., and when such payments are due. (Remember that some expenses, like ''amortization of goodwill'' are not tax deductible, and must be added back to net income to create a total that is subject to income tax.)

List your organization's expenses in each of the following categories.

Expenses related to sales:

_____

_____

_____

Seasonal expenses:

_____

_____

_____

Irregular expenses:

_____

_____

_____

Expenses related to headcount:

_____

_____

_____

Scheduled expenses:

_____

_____

_____

EXAMPLE OF A DEPARTMENTAL TRAVEL BUDGET

CORPORATE PUBLICATIONS DEPARTMENT, XYZ CORPORATION
TRAVEL BUDGET
(1993)

	JAN	FEB	MAR	(OTHER MONTHS)	TOTAL OR AVG
BASIC STATISTICS					
NUMBER OF TRIPS	1	2	4	(Insert figures for	26
AVERAGE DAYS PER TRIP	3	3	3	other months	3
NUMBER OF DAYS OUT	3	6	12	here.)	78
EXPENSE CALCULATIONS					
AIRFARE EXPENSE PER TRIP	$750	$750	$750		
TOTAL AIRFARE EXPENSE, ACCT # 4102	*$750*	*$1,500*	*$3,000*		*$19,500*
CAR RENTAL EXPENSE PER DAY	$50	$50	$50		
TOTAL CAR RENTAL EXPENSE, ACCT # 4103	*$150*	*$300*	*$600*		*$3,900*
LODGING EXPENSE PER DAY	$75	$75	$75		
TOTAL LODGING EXPENSE, ACCT # 4104	*$225*	*$450*	*$900*		*$5,850*
TAXI, TOLLS, MISC. PER DAY	$25	$25	$25		
TOTAL MISC. TRAVEL EXPENSE, ACCT # 4105	*$75*	*$150*	*$300*		*$1,950*
MEAL ALLOWANCE PER DAY	$40	$40	$40		
TOTAL MEAL EXPENSE, ACCT # 4106	*$120*	*$240*	*$480*		*$3,120*
TOTAL TRAVEL EXPENSES	*$1,320*	*$2,640*	*$5,280*		*$34,320*

DETAIL OF TRIPS

MONTH	EMPLOYEE	REASON	ORIGIN	DESTINATION
JAN	PILAR VEGAS	ANNUAL CONVENTION	PINECHIP, OH	ATLANTA, GA
FEB	JOE SMITH	AUDIT PRINTING PLANT	PINECHIP, OH	DENVER, CO
	JANICE HOPKINS	CONTRACT NEGOTIATION	PINECHIP, OH	SAN FRANCISCO, CA
(ETC)				

EXAMPLE OF AN OVERHEAD BUDGET

SMITH CONCRETE BIRDBATHS, INC.
OVERHEAD BUDGET
1993

	JAN	FEB	MAR	(OTHER MONTHS)	FULL YEAR
• OFFICE SUPPLIES EXPENSE IS A FUNCTION OF THE NUMBER OF OFFICE EMPLOYEES AND DAYS WORKED.					
NUMBER OF OFFICE EMPLOYEES	2	2	2	(Insert	2.5
NUMBER OF BUSINESS DAYS	20	20	25	figures for	260
OFFICE EMPLOYEES TIMES BUSINESS DAYS	40	40	50	other months	650
COST OF OFFICE SUPPLIES PER EMPLOYEE PER DAY	$5.00	$5.00	$5.00	in this	
OFFICE SUPPLIES EXPENSE ACCT. # 6203	$200	$200	$250	range.)	$3,755
• JANITORIAL SUPPLIES EXPENSE IS A FUNCTION OF THE NUMBER OF DAYS THE BUSINESS IS OPEN.					
BUSINESS DAYS	20	20	25		260
COST OF JANITORIAL SUPPLIES PER BUSINESS DAY	$10.00	$10.00	$10.00		
JANITORIAL SUPPLIES EXPENSE, ACCT#6205	$200	$200	$250		$2,646
• MISC. OPERATING EXPENSE IS A FUNCTION OF THE NUMBER OF BIRD BATHS SOLD.					
NUMBER OF BIRD BATHS SOLD	500	500	625		6,500
MISC. OPERATING EXPENSE PER BIRDBATH	$3.00	$3.00	$3.00		
MISC. OPERATING EXPENSE, ACCT # 6207	$1,500	$1,500	$1,875		$20,468
• ELECTRICITY EXPENSE IS A FUNCTION OF THE SEASON, OF CHANGE IN USE, AND OF CHANGE IN RATES.					
ELECTRICITY EXPENSE LAST YEAR	$150	$160	$140		$2,750
EXPECTED CHANGE IN AMOUNT USED	0%	2%	2%		
EXPECTED INCREASE IN ELECTRICITY RATES	0%	0%	5%		
ELECTRICITY EXPENSE, ACCT # 6305	$150	$163	$150		$2,923
• MISC. ADMINISTRATIVE EXPENSE IS A FUNCTION OF SCHEDULED EXPENSES AND PAST HISTORY.					
BUSINESS LICENSE EXPENSE LAST YEAR	$500	$0	$0		$500
INSURANCE EXPENSE LAST YEAR	0	2,000	0		2,000
TOTAL LAST YEAR	$500	$2,000	$0		$2,500
EXPECTED CHANGE	2%	3%	0%		
MISC. ADMIN. EXPENSE, ACCT#7000	$510	$2,060	$0		$2,570
TOTAL OPERATING EXPENSES	$2,560	$4,123	$2,525		$32,362

EXAMPLE OF A SELLING EXPENSE BUDGET

SMITH CONCRETE BIRDBATHS, INC.
SELLING EXPENSE BUDGET
1993

	JAN	FEB	MAR	(OTHER MONTHS)	FULL YEAR
• SALES COMMISSIONS ARE A FUNCTION OF SALES DOLLARS.					
EXPECTED NUMBER OF BIRDBATHS SOLD	400	400	500		6,000
AVERAGE PRICE PER BIRDBATH	$50.00	$50.00	$50.00		
SALES DOLLARS	$20,000	$20,000	$25,000		$317,000
COMMISSION PERCENT	7.5%	7.5%	7.5%		
SALES COMMISSIONS, ACCT#2100	*$1,500*	*$1,500*	*$1,875*		*$24,518*
• PACKAGING EXPENSE IS A FUNCTION OF THE NUMBER OF BIRDBATHS SOLD.					
EXPECTED NUMBER OF BIRDBATHS SOLD	400	400	500		6,000
PACKAGING EXPENSE PER BIRDBATH	$1.25	$1.25	$1.25		
PACKAGING EXPENSE, ACCT#2200	*$500*	*$500*	*$625*		*$7,500*
• FREIGHT EXPENSE IS A FUNCTION OF THE NUMBER OF BIRDBATHS SOLD.					
EXPECTED NUMBER OF BIRDBATHS SOLD	400	400	500		6,000
AVERAGE FREIGHT PER BIRDBATH	$0.75	$0.75	$0.75		
FREIGHT EXPENSE, ACCT#2300	*$300*	*$300*	*$375*		*$4,690*
• SALES RETURNS ARE A FUNCTION OF SALES DOLLARS.					
EXPECTED SALES DOLLARS	$20,000	$20,000	$25,000		$317,000
EXPECTED PERCENT OF BATHS RETURNED	3%	3%	3%		
SALES RETURNS, ACCT#1500	*($600)*	*($600)*	*($750)*		*($9,510)*
• IN THIS BUSINESS, ADVERTISING IS A SCHEDULED EXPENSE.					
PRINT ADVERTISING	$5,000	$0	$0		$5,000
RADIO ADVERTISING	0	1000	0		1,000
TV ADVERTISING	5000	1000	0		9,000
OTHER ADVERTISING & PROMOTION	200	200	200		2,400
MISC. ADMIN. EXPENSE, ACCT#7000	*$10,200*	*$2,200*	*$200*		*$17,400*
TOTAL EXPENSES RELATED TO SALES	**$11,900**	**$3,900**	**$2,325**		**$44,598**

SUMMARY OF PART 9

Many expenses have relationships with other figures that can be used to plan them: sales, business days, headcount, etc. Travel expenses can be planned after a travel policy is set. *Scheduled* expenses are already planned. *Seasonal* expenses must be planned by studying the historical expense pattern. *Irregular* expenses occur from outside causes, but can be detected by studying monthly statements. Check with professionals for advice on forecasting tax and interest expense.

10

How to Budget Depreciation Expense

What is depreciation? Your business may own buildings, machinery, equipment, etc., that it uses to produce income over a number of years. These are known as *capital assets*. A building which houses a cabinet shop, for example, may produce income for 40 years. Accountants say that each year, only a part of the total cost of such capital assets can be called an expense, more specifically, a *depreciation* expense.

The total original cost of all such assets is usually called *property, plant and equipment* on the balance sheet. The amount of depreciation charged off so far is called *cumulative depreciation expense*. *Depreciation expense*, on the income statement, is the amount charged against the business for that particular period.

The entire cost of an asset cannot be written off, since it will always have a *salvage value*. Generally, depreciation expense is: the original cost of an item, less salvage value, divided by useful life. A piece of equipment costing $1,000, with a salvage value of $100 and a useful life of 60 months, would cause a business to incur a depreciation expense of (1,000 − 100)/60 or $15 per month.

DEPRECIATION EXPENSE IS COMPLEX

Depreciation is a little more difficult to plan than other expenses. Here's why:

▶ **Depreciation is cumulative.** It depends on two things: the assets the firm already owns, and those it intends to buy. The depreciation plan is the sum of both, and the effect is cumulative. An asset placed in service today affects the depreciation plan until it is fully depreciated.

▶ **Good depreciation plans are detailed.** Depreciation is a function of almost everything the company owns, which may be thousands of items. The only way to get a precise estimate is through the accounting software, or a custom program.

▶ **Depreciation expense is calculated many ways.** The examples in this book use the "straight-line method." Other methods allow a business to recognize "more depreciation earlier," which minimizes taxes. However, straight-line depreciation is useful because it is simple, and because many large businesses use it on management financial statements.

For these reasons, it is always best to consult finance professionals before planning depreciation expense. Their software may be able to project depreciation for you, and they can explain the depreciation method used in the organization.

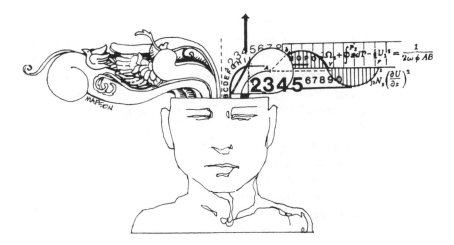

MINIMUM INFORMATION YOU WILL NEED

At a minimum, planners need depreciation information that looks like this:

Asset Class	Salvage Value	Useful Life	Depreciation Method
Land	(none)	(not applicable)	(none)
Buildings	10%	20 years	straight-line
Equipment	20%	5 years	straight-line

Land is not used up or worn out, so no depreciation is recognized.

Using the above policy, to calculate monthly depreciation for a new building: deduct 10% from the original cost, and divide the remainder by (20 × 12) or 240 months. (Remember, this is just an example. Your policy will be different.)

In the spaces below, list the classes of assets on your firm's balance sheet. For each, identify the salvage value, useful life, and depreciation method.

Asset Class	Salvage Value	Useful Life	Depreciation Method
_____	_____	_____	_____
_____	_____	_____	_____
_____	_____	_____	_____

For each asset class, what kind of capital spending do you foresee over the next few years?

_____

_____

_____

_____

_____

_____

QUICK ESTIMATES OF DEPRECIATION EXPENSE

Managers sometimes have to use rough estimates. Suppose the accounting system and finance people can't help. The only tools available are summarized financial statements, and knowledge of what new capital assets will be bought. Here is a way to estimate depreciation expense.

- First, estimate ongoing depreciation for existing assets.

- Then calculate additional depreciation caused by new capital investments.

- Last, total them to get the depreciation expense plan.

This method is used in the example on the following page.

> **PLANNER'S RULE #16:**
>
> **AT SOME LEVEL OF ACCURACY, YOU ARE ALWAYS CORRECT.**

EXAMPLE OF A DEPRECIATION BUDGET

Depreciation expense is a function of the assets you already own plus new purchases. In this example, line (i) would be carried forward to the income statement as "depreciation expense" while line (k) would be carried to the balance sheet as "cumulative depreciation." (Be careful about historical depreciation. Changes such as completing depreciation on a large portion of your assets can cause it to change.)

AMALGAMATED INDUSTRIES, INC.
BALANCE SHEET DETAIL, continued
1995

	STARTING	JAN	FEB	MAR	(OTHER MONTHS)	DEC
(a) CAPITAL SPENDING (plan)		$1,000	$5,000	$500	(Insert	$500
(b) SALVAGE VALUE (history)		$100	$500	$50	figures for	$50
(c) DEPRECIABLE VALUE (a minus b)		$900	$4,500	$450	other	$450
(d) USEFUL LIFE IN MONTHS (policy)		60	60	60	months	60
(e) ADDITIONAL EXPENSE EACH MONTH (c/d)		$15	$75	$8	here.)	$8
(f) CUMULATIVE EFFECT (e, carried forward):						
JANUARY CAPITAL SPENDING		$15	$15	$15		$15
FEBRUARY CAPITAL SPENDING			75	75		75
MARCH CAPITAL SPENDING				8		8
APRIL CAPITAL SPENDING						8
MAY CAPITAL SPENDING						8
JUNE CAPITAL SPENDING						8
JULY CAPITAL SPENDING						8
AUGUST CAPITAL SPENDING						8
SEPTEMBER CAPITAL SPENDING						8
OCTOBER CAPITAL SPENDING						8
NOVEMBER CAPITAL SPENDING						8
DECEMBER CAPITAL SPENDING						8
(g) DEPRECIATION FROM NEW SPENDING		$15	$90	$98		$170
(h) DEPRECIATION PER MONTH (history)		$500	$500	$500		$500
(i) NEW DEPRECIATION EXPENSE (g + h)		$515	$590	$598		$670
(j) BEGINNING CUMULATIVE DEPRECIATION (previous (k))		$30,000	$30,515	$31,105		$36,775
(k) ENDING CUMULATIVE DEPRECIATION (i + j)	$30,000	$30,515	$31,105	$31,703		$37,445

SUMMARY OF PART 10

Depreciation expense is a way to charge off the cost of an asset against the earnings it produces. Planning depreciation expense is complicated because it depends on existing assets as well as new assets which are purchased. To plan depreciation on new assets, it is necessary to know the cost of the assets, the asset class, the useful life, the salvage value, and the depreciation method. It is possible to estimate depreciation expense, but the most accurate method is to get actual projections from the accounting system (if available).

11

Balance Sheet and Cash Plans

Who should read this section? Of the people who use this book, most are concerned with planning income statements (or departmental expense statements). In a corporate setting, the balance-sheet plan is usually done by finance professionals. Small businesses either have no balance-sheet plan or they rely on their accountants. However, that is changing.

In Corporations. As always, regions and departments are being evaluated by the extent they maximize income (profit centers), or minimize expenses (cost centers). However, there are trends to also evaluate them on the return they generate on the assets they use, the cash and working capital they require, etc. That requires skill in balance-sheet planning from everyone involved.

In Small Business. Balance-sheet planning allows a company to know where its cash is coming from, where it is going, and what financing will look like. It helps predict liquidity crises due to seasonality of sales and working capital.

But there is a price. Balance sheets are a little more complicated than income statements to plan. To do a good job, most people should seek help from finance professionals.

However, this part of the book will help. It provides a good overview of the process. For those already planning balance sheets, some of the insights may make their task easier and their models a little more sophisticated. Also, it is a good background for dealings with finance professionals.

BALANCE SHEET AND CASH FLOW OVERVIEW

A balance sheet is a statement of the *assets* a business owns, the things it uses to produce income. Assets are usually grouped this way:

- *Current Assets*—cash, inventories, accounts receivable, investments, etc.
- *Property, Plant, and Equipment*—land, buildings, office furniture, production equipment, autos, etc.
- *Other Assets*—things like goodwill, intangibles, etc.

The balance sheet also shows where the money came from that was used to buy those assets. If it came from outsiders, it is called a *liability*. If it came from the owners, it is called *equity*. Since every item of business assets was bought with funds from either outsiders or owners, assets always equal what the outsiders invested (liabilities), plus what the owners invested (equity).

The balance sheet is sometimes called a "statement of financial position." It shows what a business owns at a particular point in time, such as the end of the year or the end of the month. On the other hand, income and cash-flow statements show what a business did over a *period* of time, such as a month or a year.

CALCULATIONS

One way to forecast a balance sheet is to take three steps:

STEP 1. Forecast the ending balance of each account except cash.

STEP 2. Calculate the resulting cash balance, by creating a cash-flow statement.

STEP 3. Review and adjust account balances.

Each step is explained further in the next few pages.

STEP 1: FORECAST ENDING BALANCES

Every balance-sheet account requires either an estimate from some source document (''a scheduled'' balance), or a rationale for calculating that balance. A loan document listing payments and principal at the end of each month is an example of scheduled balances from a source document.

You should develop a list of strategies similar to the list below. Your own, of course, will be different.*

Assets:

- *Cash.* No rationale needed. It is the result of all the other decisions combined.

- *Accounts Receivable.* An equivalent number of ''day's sales outstanding.''

- *Inventories.* An equivalent number of ''day's cost of sales.''

- *Investments.* The result of more cash than the required minimum.

- *Other Current Assets.* Use scheduled balances.

- *Property, Plant and Equipment (Gross).* Ending balance of previous period, plus capital additions, less assets retired from service.

- *Cumulative Depreciation.* Ending balance of previous period, plus depreciation expense, less cumulative depreciation of assets retired from service.

- *Other Assets.* Use scheduled balances.

Liabilities:

- *Accounts Payable.* An equivalent number of ''days of an accounts-payable base,'' consisting of change in inventory, capital spending, and cost of sales for the period.

- *Notes Payable.* Use scheduled balances.

- *Long-Term Debt.* Use scheduled balances.

- *Liquidity Debt.* The result of too little cash to meet the minimum.

Equity:

- Ending balance, plus net income for the period, plus additional funds the owners invest, less funds the owners withdraw.

*For a brief overview of balance sheets and the financial ratios referenced below, you might want to consult another Crisp publication, *Understanding Financial Statements*, by James O. Gill.

STEP 2: CALCULATE THE CHANGE IN CASH

Cash is a major issue for balance-sheet planning. *Every change between accounts, on successive balance sheets, can be viewed as either an increase or decrease to cash.* In general:

- If assets increased, cash *went down* because it was spent to "buy" them.

- If liabilities or equity increased, cash *went up,* because more financing was added to the business.

Accountants use this relationship to build a schedule called a *cash-flow statement.* This statement is useful because it shows where cash comes from, and where it goes (sometimes it is called a *statement of sources and uses of cash*). The most useful form splits cash into three parts: cash provided by operations; cash invested in the business; and cash supplied by financing. This gives a useful picture of what the business actually does.

With two successive balance sheets, an income statement for the period, and information about capital spending and depreciation, it is possible to generate a cash-flow statement for the period. This statement allows planners to project ending cash, completing the balance sheet plan.

When the balance sheet for a particular period is complete, sometimes cash is below the minimum required to run the business. When that happens, additional cash has to be raised: it must be borrowed, invested by owners, generated from operations or squeezed from other balance-sheet accounts. Those accounts must be changed appropriately on the final plan.

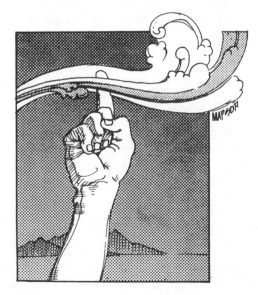

STEP 3: ADJUST THE BALANCES

With the balance-sheet and cash-flow statements complete, scan them and see if the results are reasonable. Is the seasonality of income and working capital appropriate? Do inventories grow and shrink as expected? Does cash and short-term financing make sense? Should debt be paid off? Does the business need an injection of equity capital? Can financing for future plans come from internal cash flow, or are additional sources needed? Are working capital and fixed assets the right size to support planned sales volume?

These are complex questions, and there are no obvious answers. However, the answers start with good balance-sheet plans. Adjust the balance-sheet projections as required.

Who in your organization is responsible for balance-sheet management?

_____

In your organization, who is responsible for policies in the following areas? What mechanisms exist to keep these key areas under control, and in compliance with plan? Write your answers in the spaces below.

	Responsible	**Control Mechanism**
Accounts payable	_____	_____
Accounts receivable	_____	_____
Inventory	_____	_____

AN ASIDE TO COMPUTER USERS

Many people build plans on computers. However, at the heart of balance-sheet plans is a circular relationship which makes this hard. In a nutshell:

> One source of cash is net income. But if cash is too low, companies borrow, and that changes net income (through taxes and interest). This in turn changes cash, which changes net income, which changes borrowing, which changes net income again, etc.

The relation is circular, and spreadsheets can give false readings when they contain circular references.

One trick to avoid it: Do a sequence of five or six simple cash flows—operating income, borrowing, tax, interest, cash shortfall. Feed the cash shortfall into each succeeding section. Cash shortfall will converge to zero, and the results can be used as direct estimates in the balance-sheet and cash-flow statements.

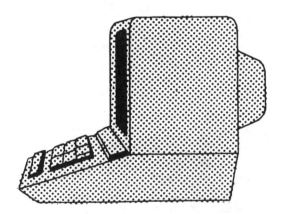

EXAMPLE OF A BALANCE SHEET BUDGET

Balance sheets show what was paid to buy the assets of the firm, and who supplied the funds: investors (liabilities), or owners (equity). Balance sheet accounts either fluctuate with business operations (inventory, receivables, payables, etc.) or are scheduled expenses like other assets, other current assets, term debt, etc.

AMALGAMATED INDUSTRIES, INC.
BALANCE SHEET PLAN
1995

	START	JAN	FEB	MAR	(OTHER MONTHS)	DEC
ASSETS						
CASH	$10,000	$10,267	$12,209	$2,402	(Insert	($1,336)
ACCOUNTS RECEIVABLE	44,000	47,300	52,030	56,438	figures for	45,150
INVENTORY	18,200	19,565	21,522	24,456	other	25,155
OTHER CURRENT ASSETS	2,000	2,000	2,000	2,000	months	2,000
TOTAL CURRENT ASSETS	$74,200	$79,132	$87,761	$85,296	here.)	$70,969
PROPERTY, PLANT AND EQUIPMENT	$75,000	$76,000	$79,000	$79,500		$82,000
CUMULATIVE DEPRECIATION	(30,000)	(30,515)	(31,105)	(31,703)		(37,445)
NET PROPERTY, PLANT AND EQUIPMENT	$45,000	$45,485	$47,895	$47,797		$44,555
OTHER ASSETS	$1,000	$1,000	$1,000	$1,000		$1,000
TOTAL ASSETS	$120,200	$125,617	$136,656	$134,093		$116,524
LIABILITIES AND EQUITY						
ACCOUNTS PAYABLE	$38,000	$42,996	$53,571	$55,350		$47,145
DEBT	80,000	80,000	80,000	75,000		60,000
OWNER EQUITY	2,200	2,621	3,085	3,743		9,379
TOTAL LIABILITIES AND EQUITY	$120,200	$125,617	$136,656	$134,093		$116,524

This company must further revise its plan. The negative cash balance in December means it will spend more cash than it has. Perhaps it could increase sales, reduce expenses, pay off less debt or make fewer capital investments.

EXAMPLE OF A CASH FLOW BUDGET

Cash flow statements are really just the difference between two successive balance sheets. Even accounts which do not normally appear on a balance sheet are really just detail for accounts that do. For example, "capital spending" and "depreciation" represent the difference in certain "fixed assets" accounts and "net income" is only the difference in certain "equity" accounts. Details of major components of the balance sheet forecast are on the following pages.

AMALGAMATED INDUSTRIES, INC.
CASH FLOW PLAN
1995

	JAN	FEB	MAR	(OTHER MONTHS)	DEC
CASH FROM OPERATIONS					
NET INCOME	$421	$464	$658	(Insert figures for other months here.)	$527
NONCASH EXPENSES:					
DEPRECIATION	515	590	598		670
CHANGE IN OTHER ASSETS	0	2,000	0		0
INVESTMENT IN WORKING CAPITAL:					
ACCOUNTS RECEIVABLE	(3,300)	(4,730)	(4,408)		2,150
INVENTORY	(1,365)	(1,957)	(2,934)		(5,590)
OTHER CURRENT ASSETS	0	0	0		0
ACCOUNTS PAYABLE	4,996	10,575	1,779		4,684
(a) TOTAL	$1,267	$6,942	($4,307)		$2,441
INVESTMENTS AND FINANCING					
INVESTMENTS: CAPITAL SPENDING	($1,000)	($5,000)	($500)		($500)
FINANCING:					
CHANGE IN DEBT	0	0	(5,000)		(5,000)
ADDITIONAL EQUITY INVESTMENTS	0	0	0		0
(b) NET CHANGE	($1,000)	($5,000)	($5,500)		($5,500)
NET CASH FLOW					
NET CASH FLOW (a + b)	$267	$1,942	($9,807)		($3,059)
BEGINNING CASH	10,000	10,267	12,209		1,723
ENDING CASH	$10,267	$12,209	$2,402		($1,336)

EXAMPLE OF BALANCE SHEET DETAIL

Accounts receivable are funds that other companies owe your firm for
purchases they have made. Many firms manage accounts receivable by
translating them into "days sales outstanding." This forecast method uses
that ratio to build a plan for accounts receivable. Remember, the results
should be adjusted for any changes in credit policies. A similar method is
used to build inventory plans.

AMALGAMATED INDUSTRIES, INC.
BALANCE SHEET DETAIL
1995

		JAN	FEB	MAR	(OTHER MONTHS)	DEC
ACCOUNTS RECEIVABLE						
HISTORY FROM LAST YEAR					(Insert	
(a)	SALES	$56,000	$61,600	$87,500	figures for	$70,000
(b)	ACCOUNTS RECEIVABLE	$44,800	$49,280	$52,500	other	$42,000
(c)	BUSINESS DAYS	28	28	35	months	35
(d)	DAYS SALES OUTSTANDING, (b/a times c)	22	22	21	here.)	21
PROJECTIONS FROM NEW YEAR PLAN						
(e)	HISTORICAL DSO (d)	22	22	21		21
(f)	BUSINESS DAYS	28	28	35		35
(g)	SALES	$60,200	$66,220	$94,063		$75,250
(h)	*ACCOUNTS RECEIVABLE, (e/f times g)*	*$47,300*	*$52,030*	*$56,438*		*$45,150*
INVENTORY						
HISTORY FROM LAST YEAR						
(a)	INVENTORY	$18,200	$20,020	$17,500		$22,750
(b)	COST OF SALES	$36,400	$40,040	$43,750		$45,500
(c)	BUSINESS DAYS	28	28	35		35
(d)	INVENTORY IN DAYS (a/b times c)	14	14	14		18
PROJECTIONS FROM NEW YEAR PLAN						
(e)	HISTORICAL DAYS INVENTORY (d)	14	14	14		18
(f)	BUSINESS DAYS	28	28	35		35
(g)	COST OF SALES (income statement plan)	$39,130	$43,043	$61,141		$48,913
(h)	*INVENTORY (e/f times g)*	*$19,565*	*$21,522*	*$24,456*		*$25,155*

BALANCE SHEET DETAIL (continued)

"Accounts payable" are funds your firm owes other businesses for purchases it has made. If you can figure out what you typically buy on credit, you can forecast accounts payable balances similar to the accounts receivable method on the previous page. Property, plant and equipment depends on the starting balance plus additions. Debt is a function of your agreement with your lenders. Equity is a function of the beginning balance plus net income plus additional funds invested in (or withdrawn from) the company.

AMALGAMATED INDUSTRIES, INC.
BALANCE SHEET DETAIL, continued
1995

	STARTING	JAN	FEB	MAR	(OTHER MONTHS)	DEC
PROPERTY, PLANT AND EQUIPMENT						
BEGINNING BALANCE		$75,000	$76,000	$79,000		$81,500
CAPITAL SPENDING		1,000	5,000	500		500
COST OF ASSETS PLANNED FOR DISPOSAL		0	(2,000)	0		0
PROPERTY, PLANT AND EQUIPMENT	*$75,000*	*$76,000*	*$79,000*	*$79,500*		*$82,000*
ACCOUNTS PAYABLE						
HISTORY FROM LAST YEAR						
(a) COST OF SALES		$36,400	$40,040	$43,750	(Insert	$45,500
(b) CAPITAL SPENDING		0	0	500	figures for	0
(c) CHANGE IN INVENTORY		0	1,820	(2,520)	other	4,550
(d) BASE (a+b+c)		$36,400	$41,860	$41,730	months	$50,050
(e) ACCOUNTS PAYABLE		$39,000	$44,850	$35,769	here.)	$42,900
(f) BUSINESS DAYS		28	28	35		35
(g) PAYABLES IN DAYS (e/d times f)		30	30	30		30
PROJECTIONS FROM NEW YEAR PLAN						
(h) COST OF SALES		$39,130	$43,043	$61,141		$48,913
(i) CAPITAL SPENDING		1,000	5,000	500		500
(j) INVENTORY CHANGE		0	1,957	2,934		5,590
(k) BASE (h+i+j)		$40,130	$50,000	$64,575		$55,003
(l) BUSINESS DAYS		28	28	35		35
(m) HISTORICAL DAYS PAYABLES (g)		30	30	30		30
ACCOUNTS PAYABLE, (m/l times k)		*$42,996*	*$53,571*	*$55,350*		*$47,145*
LIABILITIES						
BEGINNING BALANCE		$80,000	$80,000	$75,000		$60,000
PRINCIPAL PAYMENTS		0	5,000	0		5,000
DEBT	*$80,000*	*$80,000*	*$75,000*	*$75,000*		*$55,000*
EQUITY						
BEGINNING BALANCE (history)		$2,200	$2,621	$3,085		$8,852
NET INCOME (income statement plan)		421	464	658		527
FUNDS ADDED OR REMOVED		0	0	0		0
ENDING BALANCE	*$2,200*	*$2,621*	*$3,085*	*$3,743*		*$9,379*

SUMMARY OF PART 11

Balance-sheet planning is best left to professionals, but corporate managers and business owners should understand the methods and issues involved. Balance sheets are statements of what the business owns and how it was financed, at a particular point in time. One method of projecting balance sheets is to project the balance of each account other than cash; project cash by creating a cash-flow statement; and review and adjust the balances until they make sense. Projecting the balance of each account requires either a schedule of ending balances or a rationale for calculating each.

P A R T

12

Budget Reviews (From Both Sides)

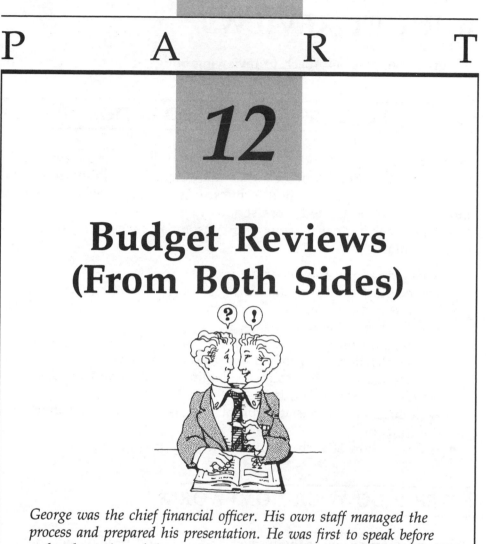

George was the chief financial officer. His own staff managed the process and prepared his presentation. He was first to speak before a closed meeting of the president and his peers. After four hours of intense grilling, he was pale, shaking, and visibly rattled.

In another company, six months after their first budget review with new owners, fully 90% of senior managers were no longer employed with the company.

Budget reviews are serious business. They can make or break your career. They can make or break your business. They are among the most important meetings you will attend in your professional career. You should take them seriously.

Few companies conduct them well.

HOW TO CONDUCT BUDGET REVIEWS

Here is a four-step approach to reviewing budgets.

STEP 1: REQUIRE A STANDARD BUDGET PACKAGE.

Create a package of standard forms that subordinates must return. Think of it as a loan application. A good format allows some flexibility, but avoids the need for different presentation formats. It guarantees the work will be done, and that it will be treated more seriously. It also allows advance preparation time, and frees budget meetings for substantial issues. At a minimum, it should contain:

- A description of the department
- The economics of the function
- The business indicators
- The financials
- History and proposed budget for all of the above
- The implications of a forced expansion in activity
- A footnote for each account explaining the data and the assumptions on which the annual total is based
- A discussion of the issues, problems, challenges, and opportunities facing the function
- A description of each position, and why it is needed

STEP 2: DO YOUR HOMEWORK.

Someone should review the budget packages and prepare additional analysis before the budget review. Here is a checklist of what they should provide:

- Proposed budget versus historical results
- Proposed budget versus similar proposed budgets
- Proposed budget for the entire company if this and all other parts are unchanged
- List of likely targets for cutting or for additional funding
- Compliance of the budget with the strategic plan

Also reread the ''Rules for Jungle Fighters'' in Part 2 of this book, and reread the strategic plan.

STEP 3: HAVE THE MEETING.

Don't retreat to an office with a stack of reports and issue decisions. Meetings provide additional information. They also provide a critical appraisal of the individual who will be spending the funds.

▶ *Consider a group review.* Have more than one individual, even peers, attend the meeting and actively review the proposed budget. However, a lot of strange dynamics will be unleashed. Control the atmosphere of the meeting to maintain a good working relationship afterward, and also to avoid a reluctance to aggressively challenge expenses because "my turn is next."

▶ *Don't do the numbers yourself.* Have someone at the meeting whose sole function is to manipulate numbers. Keep your attention focused on the issues. Keep a running tally of changes to the budget and a picture of the organization as a whole.

▶ *Talk last.* Let the individual present his or her case in its entirety, then go back over the proposal in detail. Use a schedule to assist the timid and the windy.

STEP 4: EVALUATE THE PRESENTATIONS.

Experience is important, but there are a number of techniques that will help evaluation. Here are a few:

▶ *Listen for hard spots, soft spots, and fluff.* When you lean on the plan, what collapses?

▶ *Are data and assumptions in balance?* Are they painting the future without an adequate historical base? Do they have a clear vision of the future?

▶ *Take the individual to his or her information frontier.* At some level, this individual's ability to know his or her function will break down. Is it before or after the company's information frontier? Before or after your own?

▶ *Check control capability.* If Joe gets $1 million, will he control it? Do you trust him with your checkbook?

▶ *Think like a banker.* Your subordinates are *borrowing* money from you. The burden of proof is on them, to justify their request. Have they done so?

▶ *Think like a purchasing agent.* Your subordinates are *selling* you on purchasing their proposals and services. Can outside contractors do it cheaper? Better?

STEP 4: EVALUATE THE PRESENTATIONS. (continued)

▶ *Don't take 10% off the top of everyone's budget.* This is a fundamental retreat from management responsibility. It says you do not know enough about the business to decide where cuts and increases should really go. Cuts and increases are the vital heart of an effective budget process. That is what *reallocation of resources* means. If things stay the same, why plan?

▶ *Think of an onion.* At its core, every business has certain fundamental, vital operations that drive it and determine its future, and that must be carefully managed. Like an onion, there are layers around this core that represent less-and-less-necessary, low-return activities. There will be uncertainty in your budget review decisions; it is inescapable. Just remember the onion, and make your mistakes away from the core and next to the peel.

Draw an "onion" diagram for your organization. What departments or activities lie closest to the vital core? What are closest to the expendable peel? Is your department a "core" function, or a "peel" function?

How can you redefine your mission to get closer to the core?

_____

_____

Recall your last budget review. Identify the areas where communication broke down.

_____

_____

What was the effect of these breakdowns?

_____

_____

How could they be avoided in the future?

_____

_____

HOW TO PARTICIPATE IN A BUDGET REVIEW

Successfully surviving a severe budget review requires the ultimate in management sophistication. Preparation pays. Here is a checklist you may find useful.

✔ **Know the "enemy."** Read the previous section, "How to Conduct Budget Reviews."

✔ **Know external issues.** What major issues face the company? Is it gearing up for massive expansion? Cutting costs to handle debt? What is happening with competitors? These issues are likely to color the way a presentation is received, and it should be prepared with them in mind. If reviewers are unfamiliar with external issues, be prepared to educate them.

✔ **Know internal issues.** One of the major issues is whether the CEO has a background in your functional area. If so, expect more involvement and tougher goals. (On the other hand, it may be easier to advance new projects.) If you are one of many, say one region out of four, how does it compare to the others? Who is the best? Worst? Why? How does your function compare to last year? The year before? What future trends affect your function? How are you positioned for the future? Can you converse intelligently, at *all* levels of detail down to the information frontier? How about beyond? If you are forced to reduce, what goes? If you are forced to expand, what's needed? What is the cost of substituting outside contractors for your department?

✔ **Know your business.** Is the budget still a cloud of confusing statistics? Can you talk off the top of your head about important issues? (Surprisingly, after spending a great deal of time assembling a budget, managers often fail to study what they have done.) The strategic plan looked at the forest; the annual operating plan looked at the trees. Can you still see the forest? Allow time to study the final plan and anticipate the reactions it will receive.

✔ **Prepare yourself.** Emotional preparation for the stress of a review is vital for your own well-being, as well as for the success of your budget. Manage time to keep balance in your life. Don't put off preparation so long that it interrupts your personal routine. Nothing spells incompetence like a presentation given after three sleepless nights of maximum, number-crunching effort.

HOW TO PARTICIPATE IN A BUDGET REVIEW (continued)

✔ **Polish-up presentation skills.** A budget review is really a speech. Do your skills need a tune-up? Do it before the process begins.

✔ **Keep your perspective.** Budgeting, although important, is only one of many issues you have with your superiors. For some people, budgeting brings out all their worst personality features. The wounds of the budget process will heal. Do your best and realize that the sun will still rise, your boss will smile again, and the things in life that really matter are still under your control.

✔ **Get organized.** A presentation is like a pyramid. Remember you only present the tip. Have a large back-up notebook, with lots of tabs, keyed to areas of your presentation.

✔ **Think of it as a commercial for your career.** If you have followed the planner's rules in this book, you know more about your function and you control it better than anyone else. You now have an exclusive time to show that to the people who control your career. Turn that time into a commercial for the highest management capabilities you have: your foresight, your judgment, your sensitivity to the big picture, your analysis, your creativity and your potential for promotion.

> **PLANNER'S RULE #17:**
>
> **SURVIVAL IS ITS OWN REWARD.**

List the internal and external issues facing the company that could affect how your next budget presentation is received.

Internal issues: _____

_____

External issues: _____

_____

Objectively rate your presentation skills on a scale of 1 to 10. _____

Is a tune-up necessary before your next budget presentation? _____

Identify the weakest area of your last budget presentation. _____

What steps should be taken to remedy that weakness in the future? _____

_____

SUMMARY OF PART 12

Budget reviewers benefit from a four-step approach: require a standard package, do your homework, actually have the meeting and evaluate the presentations. Budget presenters should know internal and external issues and their own particular business issues. Psychological preparation, presentation skills and organization are important. Properly executed, a budget review can be a strong commercial for your business career.

P A R T

13

Planning and Executing a Budget Process

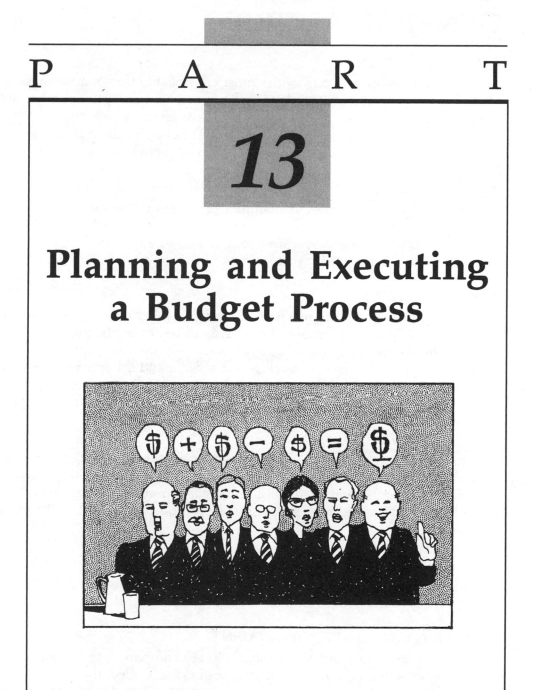

This part is for individuals who are responsible for *independent creation* of a budget process. This happens in two ways: either a manager is responsible for a departmental plan (and does not have specific rules to follow), or he or she is charged with design of a company-wide budget process from scratch. Here are some thoughts that may be useful in either case.

GENERAL ADVICE

▶ **PLAN THE PLAN.**

A planning process is one of the most controllable things a business can do. There is no reason for planning to become an exceptional contributor to overhead expense, or to require excessive effort. Make the process itself an outstanding example of good planning. Keep the calendar loose enough to allow others flexible scheduling of their planning effort.

▶ **PLANNING IS A MEANS, NOT AN END.**

There are many examples of planning processes out of control—businesses where planning becomes more important than basic operations. Planning is overhead—necessary overhead, but still overhead. Good planning is minimized. Good planning never gets in the way of operations.

▶ **KEEP IT FRIENDLY.**

Since plans are about hard numbers and painful choices, those managing the process should bend over backwards to be warm, fuzzy, and accommodating. Help the people who are helping you. Assemble common data everyone will need. Develop and share standard spreadsheet templates and master planning models. The truth is, budgets scare people. So the more severe the content, the friendlier should be the delivery.

▶ **GET THE RIGHT TOOLS.**

Many accounting packages have budgeting features, and there are many tools around. But there is one hard reality: the personal computer was built for planning and budgeting. Personal computers, spreadsheet software and trained people are so easy to find, that it is hard to justify other tools.

▶ **CONTROL WIGGLE ROOM.**

Don't allow each layer in the organization to add wiggle room. Keep wiggle room in special "budget centers" (see Part 14).

▶ **HAVE A CATCH-ALL DEPARTMENT.**

A good plan is fair and motivational. Every company has "trash" accounts and charges that no one is really responsible for. Collect them in an overhead department and assign it to a senior manager. Keep departmental budgets an accurate reflection of the activities which managers actually control.

► **HAVE A BUDGET PHILOSOPHY.**

Decide on a definite philosophy—how departments will be evaluated, etc. Communicate that information to everyone, early. Ignore the budget fad-of-the-month. Simple is a lot better than complex. Make the process a *facilitator of talented managers*—give them freedom and tools and require only clarity in return. Try not to limit the talent which can surface in the process, especially not for the sake of calculations.

► **MINIMIZE DAMAGE.**

Bad processes damage companies. Sometimes it takes months to rebuild the trust and credibility that a bad process can destroy. Remember, the planning process is a *means*.

► **GOOD PLANNING ISN'T CREATED—IT GROWS.**

It is impossible to implement a good process immediately. It *is* possible to destroy an organization by force-feeding a superb budget process for which it is not ready. Always consider how much planning-process growth an organization can tolerate in the coming year.

> **PLANNER'S RULE #18:**
>
> **THE PRESIDENT GETS ALL THE WIGGLE ROOM—EVERYONE ELSE MUST BE ACCURATE.**

Assess the tools available for your planning process on a scale of 1 to 10. ____

How can they be improved? _____

_____

How does the planning process affect morale in your firm? _____

_____

How could negative impacts be reduced? _____

_____

In your experience, under what circumstances has a planning process interfered with basic operations? _____

_____

How could that have been avoided? _____

_____

SUMMARY OF PART 13

Good budget processes are shining examples of good planning. Good planning never interferes with operations, and it is minimized, as all overhead should be. Wiggle room is the prerogative of the president; all others must be accurate. Since planning involves tough decisions, participants should make a special effort to be friendly and accommodating, and to minimize any damage to morale and teamwork. Good planning takes time.

14

How to Create an Adjusted Plan

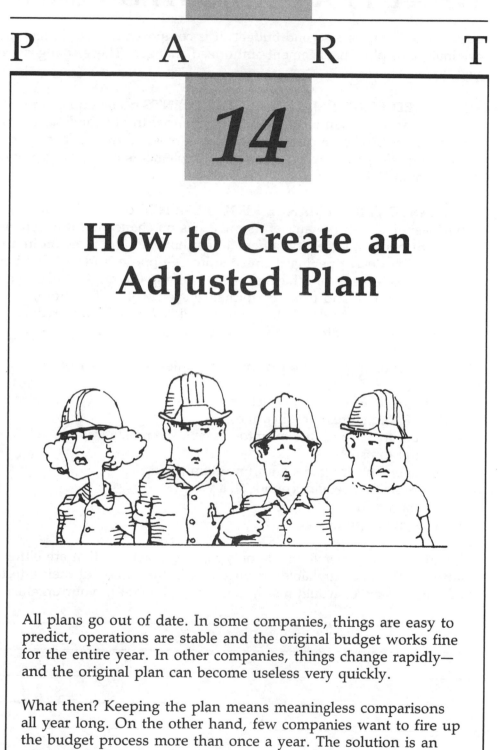

All plans go out of date. In some companies, things are easy to predict, operations are stable and the original budget works fine for the entire year. In other companies, things change rapidly—and the original plan can become useless very quickly.

What then? Keeping the plan means meaningless comparisons all year long. On the other hand, few companies want to fire up the budget process more than once a year. The solution is an *adjusted plan*.

WHAT IS AN ADJUSTED PLAN?

An adjusted plan is a second budget. It is composed of two things: the original plan, plus management-authorized changes. These changes are of two types:

INCREASED PERFORMANCE REQUIREMENTS occur under three circumstances: when a company is in financial trouble and *has* to improve performance; when a company receives a massive turn of good fortune, a so-called *windfall*; or when a company implements cost-saving programs and wants to *bank the resulting savings.*

DECREASED PERFORMANCE REQUIREMENTS occur when part of a business, through no fault of its own, has no chance to fairly achieve its plan. Suppose a large city suffers an earthquake, and a region in a national chain must delay opening planned stores. Suppose, further, that bonuses are paid as a result of achieving plan. Keeping the original plan would reduce incentive and make performance even worse. Therefore, management might decide to grant formal *budget relief,* and reduce planned performance accordingly.

Here is a list of some of the reasons companies may adjust plans:

- Opening new stores, product lines, etc.
- Closing old stores, product lines, etc.
- Temporary closing due to unforeseeable circumstances
- Natural disasters
- Management programs with uncertain timing
- Programs that require confidentially
- Reorganizations
- Cost-saving programs

Adjustments are generally made only for circumstances that are either unforeseeable, uncontrollable, or uncertain in the timing of their effects. What circumstances would justify changing a budget in your organization?

_____

_____

_____

_____

_____

_____

"RUNNING THE VARIANCE"

There is no difference between measuring performance against an adjusted plan, and excusing a budget variance. An adjusted plan *formally* excuses a variance, and gets it out of the way for the rest of the year. It has two advantages.

1. Future evaluation of performance vs. plan is easier and more obvious.

2. Managers cannot continually hide behind the same list of excuses for poor performance.

ADJUSTED PLANS AND WIGGLE ROOM

Adjusted plans are a way to formally manage and recognize wiggle room.

A business can be viewed as a series of contracts: first, between the president and the bank, owners or board; second, between the president and vice-presidents; and so on through the organization.

At the highest level, there is no wiggle room, and it is not possible to adjust the plan. Adjusting a plan with creditors is called bankruptcy. Adjusting a plan with a board of directors is called finding a new position.

Senior managers create wiggle room by negotiating a higher level of performance from their organization than they negotiate with their board or financiers. Adjusted plans (or excused budget variances) are the means by which they share this wiggle room with their organizations.

Banks don't care about excuses; they want loan payments made. No adjustment is possible for *that* plan. However, the company president realizes that adjusting his vice-president's plan will maintain motivation, and so will make the *other* plan more secure.

All of this comes together to give higher-level positions looser control but higher standards of performance.

How is wiggle room shared across the hierarchy of your organization?

_____

_____

_____

_____

_____

_____

MANAGING ADJUSTED PLANS

Most people are familiar with the terms *profit center* (a department that maximizes income) and *cost center* (a department that minimizes expenses). Adjusted plans require a third type: a budget center.

Budget centers are departments that never incur expenses. They only hold budget, for transfer into other departments, when adjustments are authorized.

Budget centers make wiggle room explicit. For example, a budget center might hold budget reductions that will occur when a confidential cost-cutting program is unveiled. When it occurs, the budget reductions are transferred from the budget center to the appropriate cost or profit center.

At the highest level, the plan never changes: the sum of budget, cost and profit centers is always the same. Senior management always knows where it stands with respect to the plan that cannot change.

However, at lower levels, the changes have meaning:

- After implementation, the cost or profit center budgets are always fully adjusted for the confidential program. Any variance is real and meaningful, and should be acted upon.

- The budget center's budget should always be zero in the current month, if all has gone according to plan (if it has all been transferred out to profit or cost centers). Any budget which does show (for the current month), measures the effect of executing the program either faster or slower than planned.

DISADVANTAGES OF ADJUSTED BUDGETS

There are several drawbacks to adjusted budgets.

- Philosophically, some senior managers allow no uncertainty. For example, if a hurricane strikes, they may feel that the profit lost should be made up elsewhere.

- Adjusted budgets also take time and effort from the finance group. Adjustments must be booked, summarized and reviewed with the same care that goes into accounting for actual results. A reasonably sophisticated group of controllers or planners is necessary. A computerized accounting system that allows multiple plans is also required.

SUMMARY OF PART 14

Adjusted plans are created in companies where circumstances change so quickly that the original plan is soon outdated. Adjusted plans have the effect of permanently excusing a variance from the original plan. Adjusted plans are a formal means for senior management to share wiggle room with other parts of the organization. Budget centers are departments that have budget but no actual expenses. They are required to properly manage adjusted budgets. Adjusted budgets require significant effort by the finance function, as well as computerized accounting systems capable of handling multiple budgets.

P A R T

15

Forecasting and Controlling Results

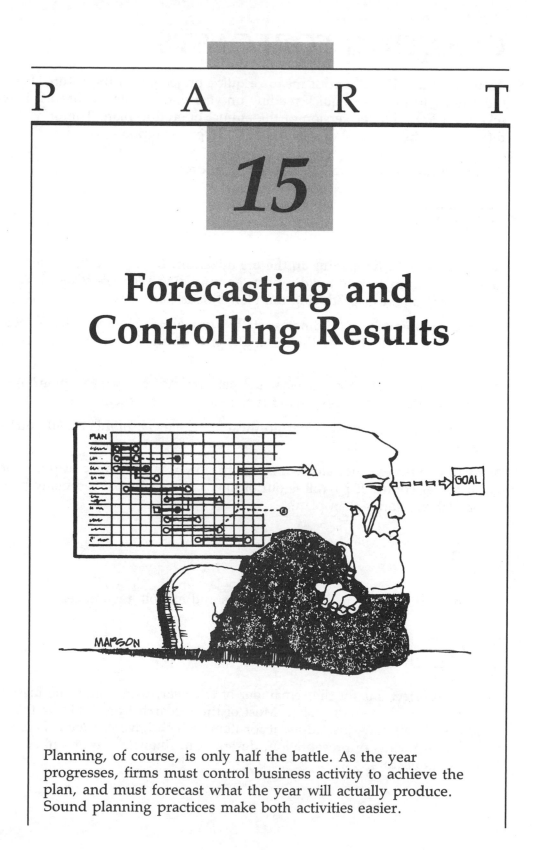

Planning, of course, is only half the battle. As the year
progresses, firms must control business activity to achieve the
plan, and must forecast what the year will actually produce.
Sound planning practices make both activities easier.

CREATING FORECASTS

As used in this book, *forecast* means a quick projection of the future. It is often done to provide a quick reading on year-end results. A forecast is really just a quicker, smaller version of the annual operating plan. The only difference is in the level of analysis and the presentation.

There are four steps to follow in creating a forecast.

STEP 1:

Research what is happening in the organization. Repeat the basic steps of gathering information to build a plan, emphasizing *what has changed*. With the experience gained in producing the plan, this is fairly easy.

► Talk to superiors, subordinates, staff, suppliers, customers, etc. Be able to explain *in words* the key themes and trends in the business, and how they have changed from plan.

► Review financials. How does actual performance compare to plan? Where are the largest variances? What is the story behind them?

► Review the economics. What do these nonfinancial numbers tell you? What is changed from plan?

► Review business indicators. If sales are down, is it because of prices or customer count? If payroll is out of line, is it because of too many people or higher salaries than plan?

STEP 2:

Develop action plans to correct problems and exploit advantages.

STEP 3:

Develop projections for the remainder of the year, using the same methods as in the annual operating plan. Most of the research from building the plan should still be good—just adjust it for items which have changed. Be sure to use all four means of presentation: description, financials, economics, and business indicators.

STEP 4:

Create the presentation. Once the analysis is done, put the forecast in presentation form. It should be just like an annual operating plan, except quicker, briefer, and more to the point. Instead of just restating the plan, which everyone has seen, a forecast should focus mostly on *variances*—areas where actual results differ from plan. Financial schedules should show the entire year on the page, with actual results for the months available, and forecast results in the following columns.

Companies vary in the forecast effort they expect. Obviously, organizations that are far from plan have much more work to do than those that are close.

When forecasts are created in your firm, what level of effort is required?

_____

How are the figures used? _____

Do you consider the level of effort appropriate? _____

Why or why not? _____

_____

USING PLANS TO IMPROVE BUSINESS CONTROL

Many companies lose a valuable benefit when they create a plan, put it on the shelf, and go to other things. Plans are an outstanding means of controlling business activities, *provided they are used.*

▶ **Spread the word.** It is important for everyone to know how the organization is doing versus plan. How? Here are two ideas:

- Make information about plan performance part of routine staff meetings, *at all levels*. Cover the company as a whole, as well as the particular department.

- Create large graphs of business indicators for each function, and post them in conspicuous locations in the department. Update regularly.

What means of distributing plan performance information exist in your firm?

_____

_____

How could these means be changed to make the information more visible and widespread?

_____

_____

▶ **Tie incentives to plan performance.** Where companies take planning and control seriously, bonus programs are tied to plan performance.

▶ **Build routine control mechanisms.** Set up regular times to review plan performance and the list of annual goals. Use the fiscal managers that created the plan to monitor and explain plan variances. Push the line and level of control down to a level that is appropriate, so that individual people understand what is happening and can take meaningful action. Forecast frequently enough to keep the organization focused on its real goals.

▶ **Improve business information.** To most people this means a bigger computer and more programmers. However, many companies could benefit even from a simple, routine, manual reporting system that focused everyone's attention on the key things that they *should* be watching anyway. Is the information frontier in your organization in need of drastic advancement?

Obviously, not all plan performance information should be widespread. In your organization, what figures should be kept confidential or restricted? Why?

_____

_____

There are many steps that can be taken to improve business control, once a company decides to take planning seriously. List three ways plan performance can be used to improve business control in your organization.

1. _____

2. _____

3. _____

SUMMARY OF PART 15

Forecasts are really just smaller versions of the annual operating plan, with special emphasis given to areas where performance is different from plan. Follow the same procedures, but adjust effort accordingly. Control can be vastly improved in most firms by using the plan appropriately through the year. Distribute information about plan performance, tie incentives to it, and use it for routine information.

FINAL THOUGHTS

Sound business planning is one of the best things that will ever happen to an organization. When it occurs, it is truly magic. Organizations do more, with less, and are happier doing it.

A strategic plan that is truly visionary, an annual operating plan that really delivers the goods, an adjusted plan that maintains fairness, a forecast that forces changes—all are among the highest achievements in the difficult art of management. There is something fascinating about seeing the future.

Such results are not easy and they will not happen overnight. However, they are worth the effort; there simply is no alternative. Good luck in your efforts, and may you be highly successful in achieving your own ultimate, personal strategic plan.

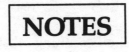

NOTES

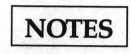

NOTES

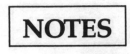

NOTES

VERN